BRIDGING

THE DIVIDE

****

THE DRIVING QUEST FOR BRINGING ABOUT AN AMALGAMATION OF DIVERSE AMERICAN CULTURES

Elbert Ransom, Jr., D. Min.

xulon
PRESS

TABLE OF CONTENTS

****

ACKNOWLEDGEMENTS

****

The propelling impetus for the writing of this book is my longing to witness and experience true brotherhood and sisterhood in the ranks of humanity in these United States of America. In preparing the manuscript, much of the data comes from the recesses of my mind, personal experiences, and research. As I reflect on my path, I am conscious of the deliberate teachings of my devoted parents, Elbert Sr. and Bernice Ransom who taught my siblings and me respect for others, and forbade us to practice any form of hate regardless of race or culture I thank my loyal devoted wife, Louise, for tolerating and understanding my many absences from our lives while completing this work, and her tireless efforts in serving as my first reader. I owe a debt of gratitude to my daughter, Angela Louise, who is a professional psychologist and a stickler for accuracy and facts, and to my sons, Gregory Elbert and Stephen Todd Jehnsen. Gregory, the history/social studies teacher, assists me in research of historical facts, and Stephen for his constant encouragement and belief that I have a story to tell.

I offer my thanks to Wilford Jackson, my prayer partner, who walks with me during the trying times.. To all the incarcerated inmates at the Alexandria Adult, and Juvenile Detention Centers, I express my gratitude. My passionate heart goes out to so many persons who helped me find my way in far distant lands of Asia, South America, Europe, Africa, Australia, South Pacific, and Scandinavia.

Finally, I fully acknowledge, and will be ever thankful for the rich social activist experience that was afforded me under the dynamic spiritual leadership of my beloved friend and mentor, the late Reverend Doctor Martin Luther King, Jr., as he took America to a new moral level and equitable respect. Most importantly, I am thankful to almighty God for sustaining my life through trying times, and never forgetting that I am his very own.

DEDICATION

****

This book is dedicated to my six grandchildren, Jordan Christopher and, Joshua Collin Jones, Addis Gideon and Damian Elias Ransom, Ava Elisabeth and Alexis Angela Jehnsen for the love and joy they add to my life. It is for them, and many like them that I wish to contribute to making this a better world. I, further, dedicate this book to the many civil rights workers and advocates with whom I shared a period of time during the turbulent 1950s and 60s for the sake of freedom and justice in our beloved America, and all of the persons who gave their lives for the cause of human equality, i.e., Medgar Evers, Viola Liuzzo, Andrew Goodman, James Chaney, Michael Schwerner, Fred Hampton, Reverend Doctor Martin Luther King, Jr., and many whose names did not make it to the marquees of justice. It is my hope that their names and contributions will be long remembered as champions of equality, and righteousness.

Again, I am humbled when I reflect upon the historical times that I spent with the late Reverend Doctor Martin Luther King, Jr. in the turbulent crossroads of American life in search of freedom and justice. To him, I dedicate this book, and my life's work for the betterment of American relational life toward God's cause of the human bond. To all of the socially deprived boys and girls I met in the favellas of Brazile, the dark villages of Africa, the jungles of the South Pacific, the rickshaw alleys of China, and the raw forgotten ghettos of America. I am passionate in remembering my beloved maternal grandmother, Eddie Harper, who insisted that on my visits to see her, I make a special visit to see an elderly white woman, whom she nursed. When I would resist, my mother reminded me that the visit was not about me but it was my grand mother's way of expressing pride in her grandson who was enrolled in college at that time. To her I happily dedicate this book

My heart is warmed and full of love for my dear siblings, William, Addie Bernice Walker, and Josie, whom I respect for reaching heights beyond their grasps as our parents encouraged. To them I dedicate this book.

PREFACE

****

The story of America to many is a continuing saga of the deliberate separation of humanity clothed in deceit, rivalry, hatefulness, racial and cultural divisions, and feint signs of harmony. This is not to negate the acts of many people of goodwill who have participated in the advancement of human freedoms for all. Our country is known by our many acts of kindness to wanting nations but not without a price. We are also known for our arrogance when we are too impatient to bother to understand other cultures of the world. I have taken advantage of the opportunity to travel extensively around the globe where I have met Europeans of means, and the people of the Baltic-Slavic countries who enjoy less of the creature comforts. I have traveled to the continent of Africa, Pacific Islands countries of (Papua New Guinea, Vanuatu, and Solomon Islands), Australia, Ireland, South Korea, China, Hong Kong, Thailand, Brazil, Ukraine, Austria, Brazil, and Turkmenistan.. Many of the countries I have visited yearn for democracy and freedom. I have been well received in every country that I have visited, because of my strong desire for world peace and brotherhood. My travels are under the auspices of the United States Department of State's Democracy and Human Rights Program as a special speaker on this same subject. My goal, as I continue these junkets, is to share my view of the commonness in human nature, and that we are not that much unalike, thereby advocating for the "oneness" of humanity.

This message, also, is of great importance to the American people as it is spread abroad.

Humanity will never fully benefit from the purpose for which we were created until we come to realize that our greatest strength is found in unity as opposed to divisions. In its diversity, America has the potential for being the world's model for racial and cultural harmony. Unfortunately, our nation has not enjoyed sustained leadership that is committed to diminishing the walls of racial, cultural, gender inequity, and politics. When my late father scrutinized his limited mobility in his environs, he said to me, "I will not be here to see the positive changes in people working together, but you will." If he were here today, he would be disappointed as we continue to live in a separatist society.

This book will discuss the many ways that we, as Americans, can contribute toward a greater distribution of the wealth of the land, the embracing and celebrating other races and cultures that are not our own, and to redefine democracy for all Americans so that the perils of human divisions become a thought of the past. We silently yearn for peace and improved understanding of what we don't know, but how wonderful it would be if more people who stand for right would speak out in support of the things that can help us move toward one nation.

Man's greed and selfishness has brought about a strain in his relationship with God. In the order of human creation, humanity was made to be in relationships with one another, and we have always lived against the grain of what God intended. We have established a social order that is not working for the common good of all humanity, because we do not know one another. There seems to be a pecking order of certain classes, races, and cultures that finds their existence at odds, and forever struggling for a place of comfort in a society of plenty. It appears that since the beginning of time human strife and conquest have been a major part of man's agenda. According to Genesis 13:8 -13, Abram and his nephew Lot parted company because of the divide between their herdsmen, both of whom claimed that there was not enough grazing land for their herds. However Abram was wise and unselfish in promoting an equitable division of the land where a peaceful decision was found to be acceptable. They could have enhanced the grazing fields and lived together in harmony. Down through the ages of time, humanity has found reasons for going their separate ways, and limiting their right to greater expansion.

When we come to understand that human existence is made to be dependent for the common good of all involved, regardless of race, culture, class, origin or ethnicity, we will have arrived at the understanding of our existence.

"BRIDGING THE DIVIDE" is not written with the desire to be one people, but, in our diversity, to emphasize and encourage the importance of the documents of American freedom the forefathers of the U.S. Constitution crafted. For the sake of peace and harmony, every race and culture should be celebrated and its history shared with others in fostering solidarity. While there might be some debate as to whether these memorable documents were meant to be racially and culturally inclusive during the eighteenth century is of no consequence, because these laws have been embraced and called into practice by all Americans here and now. At the writing of this book, the United States Congress is currently debating the rights and wrongs of immigration into the United States by citizens of far away countries. This matter was not at issue during the constitutional arguments. What is at issue is the divisiveness of the American people who have falsely lived under the 1776 motto, *"E pluribus Unum"*.

History records that the American people have never lived as one cohesive nation, which gives rise and reason for continuous discard between the races. The very soul of America is in need of healing, and especially before we attempt to save the rest of the world. Sant Kirpal Singh writes of the soul." [1]...Soul is a conscious entity; a drop of the Ocean of all Consciousness, and in its miniature capacity carries all the divine attributes of Godhood. Since it is environed by mind and matter, it has lost its heritage and forgotten its origin, the true home of the Father. The Masters come to our help to awaken us from this long slumber of ignorance. All the past Masters including Christ have been stressing the importance of this inner development of soul." It is my contention that if we believe that we were created in the image of God, it seems that we contain God's spirit within us. That special divine spirit of God has the capacity to cause the great amalgamation that is needed for our souls coming to a resting point of peace and love.

The bold work of many well-meaning organizations, and government legislators has advanced the cause of togetherness with no lasting results. The civil rights movement of the 1950s and 60s, under the leadership of Martin Luther King, Jr. made tremendous inroads in the advancement of freedom for underprivileged Americans, and much has been realized because of it. I applaud the bravery of some government legislators for their introduction of certain equitable bills that were passed, which made everyday life somewhat better for the disavowed, and disallowed people. You can legislate behavior but you cannot legislate morality. The question remains, are we a better country in equality for all citizens? I think not. We continue to struggle with equal employment opportunities, often we are baffled by the inequities in our system of justice, and equal and affordable housing remains an issue throughout most of our major cities.

We have the mechanisms in place to bring America together. What is absent is the will to do it. As far back as I can remember administration after administration has sought to assist other countries in their dire need for human rights and democracy while African American citizens lack the treatment of full citizens. As an ordained minister, I have questioned the energy that American churches put into missions abroad, when we read of the social devastation suffered by many American communities. I am aware of American churches discontinuing food and clothing closets for the needy to favor transferring the money to assist church construction in Russia, Africa, and the Caribbean. Foreign missions are a good thing, however, I am of the opinion that charity begins at home, and then spreads abroad.

The purpose of this book is to build a case for promoting togetherness in America where we are experiencing serious divisions and infractions in racial relations, political party differences, the wars in Iraq, and Afghanistan, and government and private sector corruption. We were once seen as a nation with morals, and a nation for other nations to emulate. My global travels have caused me to witness a negative response to our government, and to the arrogance and greed of the American people. We have the wherewithal to act out our moral obligations to ourselves and to the world. In order to maintain our esteemed position of leader of the free world, we must touch the resources of our souls, and aspire to being ONE AMERICA. Carol Cymbala wrote an appropriate text that has been set to a musical song entitled "Make Us One."[2]

> "Make Us One Lord, Make Us One.
> Holy Spirit, Make Us One.
> Let Your Love Flow, So the World Will Know
> We Are One With You."

This book is written as an attempt to emphasize the good that has happened in the continuous development of our native land in spite of an unforgotten sordid past, and to heighten the awareness of what more needs to be done by all Americans in helping our nation be a beacon of righteousness, mercy, justice, and love for the entire world to emulate. During the preparation and writing of this book, America has written a decisive twenty-first century historical account of the election of its first African American president, Barack Hussein Obama. He was elected at the age of forty-seven years old. He has come with a platform to change America from what it has been to what it could be to enhance the lives of all inhabitants, as well as the world. **BRIDGING THE DIVIDE** is an attempt to review our past as we move to greater levels of unity, thereby, becoming what we should be. God bless America.

INTRODUCTION

****

The pride and independence of America was first exhibited under the able leadership of John Hancock, John Adams, and Samuel Adams. These delegates from Virginia and North Carolina were charged by the Continental Congress to draft a declaration that would set them apart from England, and give them the freedom to self govern, and plan their future course of action. Therein, Congress adopted the Declaration of Independence, after minimal changes, on July 4. 1776. Since these early days, America has experienced pains making changes and modifications, but not without hope for a brighter future. We continue the path toward inclusiveness and improvement for a better America in her ability to represent and serve a great diverse population. Because of our resourcefulness, know how, and military might, we have been internationally recognized as the leader of the free world.

What has prompted me to write this book is America's continuous journey toward greatness, but not in the absence of doubt and self-criticism. Currently, the country is at a doubtful crossroad pointing blame to anyone who disagrees with his or her point of view. We have lost any sign of the collective promotion of programs and ideas that will positively benefit the country. It appears that faith and hope in sustaining America has been abandoned. The reading of **Bridging The Divide** is meant to encourage our deeds and thoughts to standing behind the very principles that were etched by the founding fathers of the Declaration of Independence: "We hold these truths to be self-evident, that all men are created equal, that they are endowed by their creator with certain unalienable rights, that among these are Life, Liberty, and the pursuit of Happiness." I believe that whenever we the people become discouraged, because of an abridgement of any one of these rights, we should reach into the depth of the recesses of our being, and elevate hope with the faith that better times can be realized.

In one of my life's experiences, my birth left me with a congenital heart problem that resulted in extreme high pertension, (high blood pressure), in the upper regions of my body and extreme low pressure in the lower region. My life expectancy was shortened by the collective knowledge of the physicians who were under the impression that they were sound in their diagnosis of the case. It took the faith and hope of my mother, who had no medical knowledge, to have her hope fulfilled in my life being renewed by her strong hope and faith rendering my life far beyond the physicians expectations. The application of improved medical technology was part of the process, and my heart problem was abated after two major surgeries fifty years apart. Those who find comfort in the greatness of hope are not usually unfettered from doubt.

The writing of this book takes into account the societal divisions within the ranks of the American people, and these divisions are not limited to race, culture, ethnic origin, but also extend to politics in government, and religion. These divisions must be addressed, if we are to continue our leadership position in the world order. Unity of mind and spirit are the two most important aspects of a people who are dedicated to victory, and that comes from collective faith and hope. According to biblical scriptures found in Matthew 12:25, Jesus taught the Pharisees about togetherness, when he said, "Every kingdom divided against itself will be ruined, and every city or household divided against itself will not stand."

Speaking to more than 1,000 delegates from the Republican Party, a hopeful President Abraham Lincoln gave his "House Divided Speech in Springfield, Illinois. In that remarkable speech, he paraphrased Jesus' statement that was more directed at the slave conditions of the time.

CHAPTER I

THE AMERICAN DIVIDE

****

When . . . you have succeeded in dehumanizing the Negro;
when you have put him down and made it impossible for him to be
but as the beasts of the field; when you have extinguished his soul
in this world and placed him where the ray of hope is blown out as
in the darkness of the damned, are you quite sure that the demon
you have aroused will not turn to rend you. . .

Abraham Lincoln

Ronald Wilson Reagan, the 40th president, did more to stymie the ongoing progress of African American social changes than any other president of the United States of America. He served as an impediment in the path of forward development of a down-trodden people seeking equal status in a racially divided America. His tenure as president depicted an evil era of undoing years of progress toward the building of an equitable society. The Reagan years were, frightfully, a time when championed civil rights gains were eroded and dismantled, with no regard for the plight of suffering African Americans or the poor. Irene Monroe, a regular contributor to "A Globe of Witnesses, wrote in her monthly online column called "Remembering Ronald Reagan's Evil Empire, March 25, 2008:

"Many religious conservatives believe that evil is born
into a person; therefore, when you remove the bad seed
you ostensibly remove the evil. However, evil exists
in it's various machinations because of systems, regimes
principalities, and yes, presidencies of domination that
allow it to give birth unchecked."[1]

President Reagan demonstrated that he was no friend to the
poor: he reduced subsidized housing which contributed to the rise
of homelessness. He was insulting enough to state that poor African
American women were "welfare queens residing in cadillacs." In
What seemed to be a war against the poor, he reduced school lunch
programs and interfered with school bussing programs, replaced
vocational schools with prisons, and registered no interest in
offering financial assistance to college students who were in need.
There are many other social atrocities that are attributed to Reagan,
such as his calloused disregard for the people who mourned the
deaths of the murderous killings of three civil rights workers, James
Chaney, Andrew Goodman, and Michael Schwerner in Philadelphia,
Mississippi where he launched his presidential campaign. Because
of the grief for the three civil rights workers murderous death, Mr.
Reagan could have shown sensitivity by launching his conservative
campaign elsewhere. It should not be forgotten that Reagan aligned
himself with the racist government of South Africa during the time
that apartheid was widely practiced. It is clear that Ronald Reagan
was not a supporter of equal rights in America, and he set the country
back many years in the advancement of positive racial relations.

Reagan, in the dismantling of left-wing social advancements,
brought in Black right-wing conservatives to assist him in his diabolical plan of disrupting the civil rights establishment. Conservative
supporters protected him from criticism for his assault on minori-
ties and the American poor. He appointed Clarence Pendleton to the
U.S. Civil Rights Commission, while pressuring the current members to resign from the Commission, rendering it impotent as an
independent watchdog. He then gave the country Clarence Thomas
with the latitude to destroy the Equal Employment Opportunities

Commission (EEOC). The Reagan years staged a retraction on many of the civil rights gains that happened before his presidency.

It doesn't take a rocket scientist to come to the conclusion that the Reagan era opposed racial equality, and he forfeited any opportunity to be placed in the annals of history as a great president of the American people. He was a great divider, which gave the Republican party their hero. At the writing of this book, America continues to be divided around racial issues, and it continues because no American President, except Abraham Lincoln, has, of his own volition, placed racial equality at the apex of the American agenda. Others acted from political or public pressure to consider such a controversial move².

A unified people give strength to their plight. Jesus taught the Pharisees about togetherness, when he said, "Every kingdom divided against itself will be ruined, and every city or household divided against itself will not stand." More than 1,000 delegates from the Republican Party on June 16, 1858 heard Abraham Lincoln give his "House Divided" Speech in Springfield, Illinois. In this remarkable speech, Lincoln paraphrased Jesus' statement that was more directed at the slave conditions of the time. He said of slavery:

"Mr. President and Gentlemen of the Convention. We are now far into the fifth year, since a policy was initiated, with the avowed object, and confident promise, of putting an end to slavery agitation under the operation of that policy, that agitation has not only, not ceased, but has constantly augmented. In my opinion, it will not cease, until a crises shall have been reached, and passed a house divided against itself cannot stand…"

Lincoln proved his strong courage during those perilous times, even if it was only to save the union. This firm statement by Lincoln would ultimately find him in the right place at the right time. Here we find ourselves in the 21st century, with the same basic struggle of the 1800s. Division is dysfunctional, and destructive.

The rest of the world once looked to America as a beaconed model that would point them in the direction of freedom, justice, and mercy. However, with the advent of high visual technology, and improved communication, the whole world is watching us in our often ill treatment of many who happen to be underprivileged.

Given the governmental collapse, and the lack of economic and educational opportunities in many third world countries, the demographics of America are currently undergoing serious change, with the migration of other cultures. If this is an accepted truth, the current racial and cultural divide will become more complex. In the face of the reality of immigration to this land of plenty, it would seem logical to get ahead of the possible problem of future assimilation by promoting a movement of unity. Such an effort can bring about better understanding of the environment, and the inhabitants therein. The problem is that we do not know one another. Currently the American divide is predicated on race, culture, religion, economics, politics, and education. These building blocks of prejudice and stereotypical behavior result in racially segregated housing and gerrymandering of school districts.

It appears that we find our comfort zones in living homogenously, which prohibits enhancement of any kind. History has taught us that sociological divisions have always been the way of life, however, this practice continues to impede our progress in growing beyond our potential. When we set limitations on social and economic development, we stymie the opportunities for further human development. Blatant ignorance promotes the barriers that separate us, and limits our true knowledge of one another to the degree of complete sociological destruction. The problem with such limited expansion and exploration is that we smother in our own boredom and likeness.

Inside The Divide of Politics

When the U.S. Constitution was framed, the focus of our forefathers was emanating power, and how state and national governments would function. There was not much emphasis on the political and electoral process. These details were to be determined by the congress and the states. However, during the presidential election of 2004, it took the action of the Supreme Court to settle the election of George W. Bush. After two hundred years plus, we have come to a point in time where we need to modify the political system so that citizens who feel that governance is not theirs will again be fully involved.

Unfortunately it appears that our system of government is propelled by greed, and special interest. Herein breeds the avenue to divisiveness. Financial contributions to legislators, who have been elected to represent our concerns, are often bribes. These bribes are so pervasive that our legislators are deeply indebted to special interests. There are many legislators of good will of the Democratic and Republican parties who work to bring an end to lobbying for self – interest.

It is interesting how labels, colors, sizes, ideologies, behaviors come to define persons of differing persuasions. While there are two major political parties, Democratic and Republican, there are countless other parties which rarely come to the fore. For years the United States has been globally recognized as a two party system. This, of course is open for challenge, because of the other listed parties. Since the 2000 presidential election we have further delineated the population division by the colors of red and blue. The red states are perceived to lean toward the Republican ticket, while the blue states lean toward the Democratic ticket. Red represents a more conservative interest, and blue states more liberal interest.

It appears that the red/blue color divide became more prevalent during the split between the voting for George W. Bush and Al Gore. Geographically, George W. Bush's red included the states across the South where racism, conservatism by another name, is played out, the Great Plains, and the Rocky Mountains. Al Gore's divide included New England, East Coast, and the West Coast. It is noteworthy to review the media's role in biased reporting, more like yellow journalism. Greed drives the biggest wedge in the political, economical, and sociological divide.

One observation is that the red states having done a poorer job in making life better for all of its citizens than blue states. It is no accident that the red state – blue state divide is indicative of a persistent racial split in the United States, and there is blatant inequity in the socio-economic status of African American citizens. When this phenomenon is taken into full account, one will readily see the divide being more than political but social as well. The red state, blue state divide is deeply rooted in an all too familiar problem of racial injustice. It would be ill advised to leave the brunt of the problem in the hands of white politicians when many of our representatives are often African American Democrats.

The political divide has become more pronounced in the wake of President Barack Obama's presidency. More pointedly, the Republican Party has demonstrated their unhappiness with President Obama's victory in 2008 by rejecting initiatives that have been introduced and advanced by him. This has caused much speculation as to motives. The Republican loss was devastating, and their actions caused legislative gridlock. While the president has extended the olive branch, there are no takers.

Divided by Faith

There is a poignant, and meaningful declaration found in the biblical book of Psalms 133. These poetic words have been reported as the words of David, who recognized his need to live in harmonious relationships with others. He wrote, "How good and how pleasant it is for brethren to dwell together in unity..." These words of inclusiveness give us hope for a time when God's people will come to full knowledge of what their rightful mission is in a world that is divided, and fraught with discord.

We live in a time where races fight against races, cultures fight against cultures, political parties against political parties, religions against religions, nations against nations, but there is one God for us all. Of the many religious faiths offered to us, we have the right to choose where we find comfort and fulfillment. Whether we choose Christianity, Islamic, Judaism, Buddhism, Hinduism, or Baha'i Faith, we have a common ground of caring for our fellow persons. This is where we can begin to explore the similarities in faiths.

The division of race and culture in America is the single most destructive impediment to realizing the true meaning of freedom. One would think that the 68,574 churches recorded across the landscape of America would have a profound persuasive bearing of the promotion of unity. The church, as we know it, has been derelict in her mission of moral leadership. Unfortunately, religion is a very guarded practice for many who are deeply reluctant to share or give up their zones of comfort.

Dr. Michael O. Emerson, Sociologist, Rice University, estimates that approximately 5.4 percent of U.S. churches are racially integrated, which, for Emerson, means no one group makes up more than 80 percent of the congregation.[3] These communities of faith were gleaned from the United States Churches Database in an effort to approximate the number of worship centers in America. If the community of faith exercised the primary obligation of ushering God's diverse people into a unified concept of living, the impact on this country would be phenomenal, and the world would take heed to such a demonstration of peace and well being.

As racial and cultural demographics change, many churches have not taken advantage of the opportunity to diversify their congregations. They continue their aged old practice of serving their own kind, and when the onslaught of newcomers relocates into a given traditional community alienation sets in from all involved. The general practice of racism in the church occurs when the church attempts integration of the races. If the pastor is brave enough to lead and support the integration effort, a certain number of people will leave, silently expressing their unwillingness to experience change.

I served as an Associate Pastor at a leading African American Baptist Church, and as the years passed during my 14 years of service, I made a decision to relocate to a predominantly white church with a White pastor. I chose this particular church for reasons of warm acceptance by the congregation, and a pastor who was not reticent in proclaiming an inclusive gospel. When my wife and I began serving, I found myself to be one of ten African American members attending at that time. Over the eleven years of my membership, several African American persons joined the church. With this personal venture, I am convinced that people who are inclined to attend church look for a spiritually fulfilling experience, regardless of demographics.

It took the prophetic mind of the Reverend Doctor Martin Luther King, Jr. to observe and articulate, " The most segregated hour in America is 11:00 AM on Sunday." America's racial history defies any great strides toward multiracial churches. Thus far, few multiracial churches are successful. Examination of the races and their church practices leads one to assume that people take religion very seriously, and worship with people of the same race. They seem to look favorably on a multiracial church if others adapt to their culture and style of worship. However, until America comes to cure the many racial inequities, i.e. economics, housing, education, and employment, the church will remain a segregated and isolated entity in a world where the church's mission is expected to enter the moral sphere of our lives. As we seek a more moral guiding principle, we must ask the question, whether we as part of the American Community of Faith will achieve the multi church community of which Dr. King dreamed in which God's people, of all races, will join and sing, with meaning, "We shall Overcome?"

One Nation and Two Flags?

A patriotic flag is a symbol of a country's identity. Nations around the globe are quite respectful to that particular symbol of pride and loyalty. The preservation of the flag is sometimes protected by the supreme sacrifice of life. It has been in history that the American flag was made by the seamstress Elizabeth Griscom Ross Ashburn Claypool, alias, Betsy Ross. The historical account of her American flag making, which was told by her grandson, quickly became legend. However, the authenticity of this story continues to be unconfirmed. What we do know is that the flag appears to have been made in 1776, and has been America's signature symbol since that time. However with the formation of the Confederate States of America in 1861, first priority of the confederate government was to create a flag for what was envisioned a new nation. Those who were commissioned to create the new flag were first urged to make something that looked like the existing United States flag, and secondly create a flag very different from the existing United States flag. Given the two schools of thought, they created a flag that resembled the United States flag, however, the stars and stripes were replaced with three bars of red and white, and seven stars which represented the seven states at that time. This flag came to be known as the first Confederate flag. Because of confusion in recognition between the United States flag and the first confederate flag, General P.G.T Beauregard suggested that the Confederate national flag be changed to something different that would eliminate confusion especially in time of battle. While the Confederate government rejected his idea, he was able to persuade them to approve a special battle flag, which would be a blue X on a red field, and the flag would have thirteen stars for the now thirteen states in the Confederacy. This flag gained widespread acceptance, and became the Confederate battle flag that is used and displayed as the Confederate flag.

The Confederate flag, in contrast to the United States flag, continues to be a point of contention between African Americans and conservatives. It is reported that it is seen by, some Southerners as a remembered symbol of Southern pride. African Americans view it as a symbol of racial separation, and white domination. The flag still remains flying from the public buildings of some Southern states. It has also been observed being used by active racist as an alternative to the American flag. This flag was thoughtfully created in time of the Civil war to distinguish the thirteen Southern states that supported slavery as a way of life.

Currently this celebrated symbol is a major part of the American divide. The differences over the Confederate flag expose the present, sometimes, heated debate about racial equality in the land of the free and the home of the brave. America has one symbolic flag the stars and stripes that represent our freedoms, and when we all come to accept this fact, we will begin to understand our true purpose of unity. Francis Scott Key and John Stafford Smith, in their collaboration in writing the National Anthem provided a great tribute to our flag: Let there be one America, one brotherhood/sisterhood, and one flag under which we stand.

" O say, can you see, by the dawn's early light,
What so proudly we hailed at the twilight's last
Gleaming, Whose broad stripes and bright stars,
thro the perilous fight, O'er the ramparts we watched,
were so gallantly streaming? And the rockets red glare,
the bombs bursting in air, Gave proof thro' the night
that our flag was still there. O say, does that star

*spangled banner yet wave O'er the land of the free
and the home of the brave?"*

This symbolic fabric represents our American values and commitment to a common purpose that makes us unique. When we absorb all that has been positively touted about the greatness of this country, we cannot help but feel the pride of a people who have contributed to her strength, even through all of the vicissitudes in becoming who we are. It is with this determination, and fortitude that we are what we are and who we are. God Bless America was my first singing solo performed in a Mississippi school- house in 1940, where my mother taught school. Today, I sing that patriotic song with wet eyes, because the words mean something to me that personalize my relationship to an ideal, though, I refuse to believe it was not meant to be inclusive.

Because of the greatness this country has come to extol, there has to be a degree of embarrassment before the world in the demonstrated practice of human relations. We have the wherewithal to be the global model in the area of fairness, equality, and human rights. It is hypocritical to pretend to be what you are not. As the world advances in modern travel, and high technology we cannot hide our actions. When we attempt to impose our values on other cultures, we render ourselves untrustworthy.

It would be far better to exercise the leadership role in putting the right practices in place, and be a living example of how to live with others who are unlike us. I truly believe the future generations will take hold of our inabilities to coexist and make this a better world order. It will not happen from our examples, but because true human survival will depend on it.

CHAPTER II

LIVING IN DISUNITY AND FEAR

****

*Unity makes strength, and since we must be strong,
we must be one.*

Grand Duke Friedrich von Baden

A profound wish for many is that God in His infinite wisdom would intervene in the ranks of the American people, in our racial and cultural diversity, and cause us to come together in human solidarity and be one. My heart weeps when I reflect on how divided we are, and how greed, racism, political corruption, and violence are destroying the very core of our existence. God's order of creation was intended for us to live in supporting and caring relationships, but we have defied His intentions, and find ourselves living in fear of one another. When God made man His intent was that man would live harmoniously with all that He made. In the divine order of the universe God created humanity to be in spiritual relationship with each other so that we would have the strength and capacity to build His kingdom on earth.

Somehow we have managed to live outside of His divine plan in efforts to pursue our own chosen path. Many of us have experienced paths that are fraught with pain, sickness, stress and disappointment. We have strayed much too far from the family of God, and have become aliens to the very principles for which we were intended. There is a poignant word by a prolific writer and poet by the name of

Sam Walter Foss. Foss understood his purpose on earth. He mused about his life among other human beings in the most diverse sense he wrote:

"Let me live in a house by the side of the road where the races of men go by. Some who are good, some who are bad, but not as good or bad as I. I sit not in the scorners seat or hurl the cynics ban, but let me live in my house by the side of the road, and be a friend to man." [1]

According to Genesis 2:18, God spoke the words, "it is not good that man should be alone," and so he placed man in the company of another being which eventually multiplied into a family of humanity. To be in communion with like minds and spirits is God's way of assuring peace and solidarity. In our celebrated human diversity, as we maximize our strength, we should not allow any self- imposed barriers to further divide us. We must overcome the walls of different languages, culture, prejudice, geography, economic class, education and gender differences. In overcoming our differences, individually and systemically, we must covenant together to enter into a new sphere of living outside of our comfort zones and discover and celebrate the good within us all.

There are many ideal approaches to ushering in a new social order, and it begins with basic inter-cultural education accompanied by universal standards of living with others who have not begun to share our values and mode of behavior. The standards of living will have to take into account a shared blending behavior model that is easily adaptable from one culture to the other. Language barriers and cultural customs can be difficult hurdles to mount, however, in a land of multiple differences, sacrifices must be realized in an effort to maintain peaceful coexistence. Communities can organize cultural study groups to learn of other cultures, facilitated intercultural/racial dialogue, intercultural food tasting, church and school sponsored dialogue. With desire and unfaltering courage, there are many creative ways to overcome the barriers that separate us from one another.

One of the biggest barriers that confront us is fear. Fear of the known and the unknown is a natural phenomenon in the lives of mortal beings. We become anxious about things that we think will bring harm to us, and we become alarmed about the evils in the unknown that we perceive will compromise us. In my reflections of fear, I have come to the conclusion that fear is a contagion that transforms rationality into irrationality, which can cause a cancerous epidemic which erodes the very essence of humanity. When I was a child, I experienced fear of the dark because I could not discern what I could not see. My imagination took flight, and caused me to conjure every manner of evil in the dark. Other times, I feared the anticipated ferocity of barking dogs. I also feared the reprimands of my parents when I was found disobedient. The experience of fear is nature's way of alarming us to the possibility of evil or pain.

Sigmund Freud, the Austrian neurologist, and founder of psychoanalysis, spoke of a person who was quite properly afraid of snakes in the heart of the African jungle, and another person who neurotically feared that snakes were under the carpet in his house. He said that many fears are real, and others are acquired. Most fears are snakes under the carpet.[2] During a time in America's most memorable economic depression and war, Franklin Delano Roosevelt, the 32nd President of these United States uttered these words in his inaugural address, "We have nothing to fear but fear itself." Fear has always been an important factor in human development. It has played an important role in our survival as humans. We continue, in the 21st century, on the road to destruction because of our greed, and racial and cultural ignorance of others who share this borrowed environment. Leaving our nagging fears behind, and turning to dreams of an increasingly secure future would better serve us. However, in the process, too many of us have become more focused on ourselves and lost our focus on community. We become engrossed in our own desires instead of considering the needs of those who never experienced a time without fear. We live in fear of the evils that we know, and the evils that we don't know about. Since the September 11, 2001 travesty and devastation of the Twin Towers, terrorism has become a household word in the world language. Not only is it a word, but a real dilemma, and a part of our everyday concern. This tragedy has changed American life drastically. We are afraid of public gatherings, the water we drink, the food we eat, the air we breathe, and the strangers we meet. Man has come to believe that the earth belongs to him, and the bona-fide rights to all of the natural resources within. The mineral rights that are in the earth, which man extracts to make powerful explosives of destruction, belong to God, and yet we fear nations that hoard and extract such minerals. Wouldn't it be better in exploring constructive ways of dialogue to work to the abatement such fear?

The bible, according to Psalm 24, tells us, "the earth is the Lord's, and the fullness thereof; the world, and they that dwell therein…" Some believe that when God created man, his intent was that man would be an obedient steward over all that He had made. He further intended for man to peacefully subdue the earth and be fruitful and multiply so that God's kingdom here on earth would be a foretaste of heaven. Henry Wadsworth Longfellow makes the point in his poem, Psalm of Life: "Tell me not in mournful numbers, life is but an empty dream! For the soul is dead that slumbers, and things are not what they seem. Life is real! Life is earnest! And the grave is not its goal; dust thou art, to dust returnest was not spoken of the soul."

Whether to preserve the union or from a benevolent heart, Abraham Lincoln braved the social, and political tempest by signing the Emancipation Proclamation in 1863. It has been reported that neither Lincoln nor the congress knew just what constitutional powers befell them in the area of human rights, but he was willing to use the powers he had to the limit. Lincoln enacted the cessation of black slavery in the United States of America, in part: Until the election of President Barack Obama , bridging of the racial and cultural divide has not been an imperative of any prior President since Lincoln.

"That on the first day of January, in the year of our Lord one thousand eighteen hundred and sixty-three, all persons held as slaves within any state, or designated part of a state, the people whereof shall then be in rebellion against the United States, shall be then, thenceforward, and forever free; and the Executive Government of the United States, including the military and naval authority thereof, will recognize and maintain the freedom of such persons,

and will do no act or acts to repress such persons, or any of them, in any efforts they may make for their actual freedom."

It was the boldness of will, and the stroke of the pen to set the course on the path of race relations for the following one hundred forty-seven years. It was one hundred years later that another sitting president to stood against the wishes of the demagogues of racial prejudice. John Fitzgerald Kennedy stood the test of time by advancing the plight of the registration of black voters in the south. He also stood with James Meredith, a black man who wanted to go to an all-white school at the University of Mississippi, but was denied admission. However, with the president's help, Meredith, under the watchful eyes of Justice Department Officers, graduated with a degree in Political Science.

Once more Kennedy exercised his power as the commander-in-chief by using the United States Army to allow two black students to enroll in University of Alabama, where the late Governor George C. Wallace bodily blocked their entrance. President Kennedy framed the perils of civil rights in a moral perspective. He said: "It is as old as the scriptures and is as clear as the American Constitution." His final bold act for justice was the enactment of The Civil Rights Act of 1963. He did not live to see the act become law, because of his assassination in November of 1963. The Civil Rights Act became law in 1964.

President Lyndon B. Johnson served as Vice President under John F. Kennedy, and became President after Kennedy was assassinated. Johnson knew of Kennedy's desire to see the Civil Rights Act become law, and he signed it into law. He remarked in his speech " the law is a product of months of the most careful debate and discussion. Our late and beloved President John F. Kennedy proposed it more than one year ago. It received the bipartisan support of more that two thirds of the members of both the House and the Senate. An overwhelming majority of Republicans as well as Democrats voted for it."

In the face of criticism and rejection, these aforementioned men blazed new paths in the continuing historical saga, because they heard and stepped to the beat of a different drummer for freedom.

Unfortunately, courage in bringing about demographic unity in America has not been a prominent agenda item for most of our presidents. The twenty-first century has ushered in the most divided times of all.

The racial progress that was made up to the nineteen sixties has slowly deteriorated beginning with the Reagan years, where there seemed to be less tolerance and respect for black social justice. The result has meant demoralization in American values. America has enjoyed or tolerated forty-three presidents who, for the most part, did not serve as advocates for civil liberties. Thereby, supporing a divided America during their tenure. Great moments in history come with bold leadership, but this has not been the case in any attempt to racially and culturally solidify America.

No president has served this country with a clean and equitable slate on civil liberties, nor do the Republican and Democratic parties enjoy a monopoly on morality in defending the principles found in the Bill of Rights. At the treatment of this subject, Samuel Walker's Book, "An Uncertain Defense: Presidents and Civil Liberties from Wilson to Bush," he alludes to an informal poll in 2006 where professional historians rated George W. Bush the worst president ever in American history.[3] One would have concluded this poll was a little advanced, especially since Mr. Bush had until 2008 to prove himself, however, it appears the informal poll was with merit.

If one wishes to examine Bush's position on certain civil liberties, you might consider the following record: According to Walker, he led an all-out assault on the separation of church and state, abortion rights and gay and lesbian rights. Threats to freedom of speech and due process protections are laden in the USA PATRIOT Act. Nothing was advanced to suggest improving race and cultural relations throughout the Bush administration.

It has been etched in the annals of history that a liberal Democratic president would boldly stand up to defend civil rights. Democratic presidents have been noted for their abhorrence in violations of civil liberties. However, between 1913 and 1921 President Woodrow Wilson's administration disallowed free speech during the First World War, however, Franklin D. Roosevelt interned 120,000 Japanese American during the Second World War.

We often refer to the good old days, when we had sustained morality, values, and great American virtues. In our reminiscence let us be realistic when it comes to making judgments about what was good and bad about the times. It would be good to review just how well past presidents have stood the test of defending civil liberties, equal protection of the law, equal protection of privacy for all citizens, and free speech. In most cases we will find that the question on presidential defense and advocacy for the civil rights for all Americans is null and void. Many of these presidential leaders were deemed good men with moral consciences, however they were ambivalent on the civil liberties issues. They found themselves swayed to the immoral side of their constituents. Were they open to sound reasoning, they could have, introspectively, asked the questions, as posed by Martin Luther king, Jr. " Cowardice asks the question, is it safe? Vanity asks the question, is it popular? Expediency asks the question, is it politic? Conscience asks the question, is it right? There comes a time when one must take a position, that is neither safe, nor popular, nor politic, but because conscience tells you that it is right."

No matter what their intentions are, our leaders are not capable of waving a magic wand to bring us together as a unified nation. It takes the will of the human spirit, and an understanding of those aspects of humanity that we have in common. The hopeful goal of taking advantage of our diversity cannot be obtained with money, nor compelling power, and most certainly, as smart as we are, technology cannot bring it into being. When we all come to acknowledge and respect the divine origin of human creation in its diversified forms we will come to appreciate what we have in common as earthly beings.

Many American people live in constant distrust of one another. They have little or no willingness to venture outside of their comfort zones. There appears to be no interest in exploring, and getting to know other human beings who don't resemble them, nor speak as they do, nor share the same skin pigmentation, or relate identical life experiences. We live day-to-day having distorted degrees of knowledge about one another, thereby constituting stereotypical fear, and dislike.

This age-old lifestyle between races and cultures, fettered by the chains of hatred and bigotry is the cancer that dominates the healing process of greater unifying possibilities for America. We are now threatened with complete nuclear destruction, because of the dispensation of reckless power in the hands of those who feel that the future belongs to them, only. America is living on the edge because of terrorist threats, trigger-happy world leaders, and the usurpation of our natural resources.

America can look back on the past few decades when we envisioned a brighter future with a flourishing economy, and improved relationships between races and cultures. The stagnant problem is born out of fear; greed; hate, and racism. We have been reduced to fear on every side. The experience of fear has ushered in the discomfort in extending ourselves in forming the beloved community. Within the rank and file of respective races and cultures, divisions are apparent, which further living counter to the purpose of human creation.

For the sake of peaceful human survival in America, our wish should be that the God of love, peace and understanding would intervene within the ranks of the American people, and cause us to come together in true meaningful solidarity and be one in spirit. Let us, also, wish that men and women would come to regard the intended sanctity of this young country and eradicate the seeds of hate, greed, political corruption, racism, and violence which is destroying the very core of our existence.

God's intended order of creation was that we live in supporting and caring relationships; somehow we have defied His intention, and find ourselves at odds with His plan for us. Unfortunately, of all of the celebrated American institutions, the Community of Faith has been much too silent on the issue of human unity, ministers fearing that they will alienate their congregations, and possibly lose members. The gospel was written as true messages for all to hear and practice. We must find creative ways to make real the family of brotherhood and sisterhood in answering our call to unify the family of God.

The May 1987 edition of National Geographic included a feature about the Arctic Wolf. The author, L. David Mech described how a seven-member pack targeted several musk-oxen calves that were guarded by eleven of their adults. As the wolves approached their quarry, the adult musk oxen bunched in an impenetrable semicircle with their deadly hooves facing out, and the calves remained safe during a long standoff with the wolves.

But then a single ox broke rank, and the herd scattered into nervous little groups. A skirmish ensued and the adults finally fled in panic, leaving the calves to the mercy of the wolves. Not a single calf survived.[4]

The Apostle Paul warned the Ephesian Elders in Acts 20 that after his departure wolves would come, not sparing the flock. In other words, wolves continue to attack and penetrate, destroying unity. When we break rank, we become easy prey. America is vulnerable, because our ranks are fractured, and our leaders are misguided, and have assisted in our ranks being broken. The mantle is in the hands of the people to assist in making us one.

The strength in our ranks comes with commitment to a unified cause that is articulated by trusted leadership which has the will of the people as the guiding compass. The American people have a history of rallying around that which is perceived as justice and righteousness. It is the strong will to survive that propels humans toward victory, and averts the agony of defeat. Working together toward a common goal fulfills the expectation of teamwork, and the successful achievement of the end product.

One of the highest levels which can be achieved by mankind, is the revealing of unity by God. Unity within the ranks of humanity achieves the depth of spirituality found in the quiet zones of our inner being. It is at these seldom visited times that we are reluctant to search our true selves because we fear that part of us that is unknown, untried, and reluctant to reveal to others.

Before we can soulfully connect with the outer limits of our being, we must find true comfort in who and what we really are. In Shakespeare's Hamlet, the profound verse, "To thine own self be true…" is an expression <u>that</u> is intended to examine ourselves before we can be true to others. Truth is a necessary part of healing our inner wounds, and allowing us to be empathetic to our fellow beings.

CHAPTER III

A NATION IN NEED OF HEALING

****

*Let new earth rise. Let another world be born.... Let a beauty
full of healing and a strength of final clenching be the pulsing in
our spirits and our blood. Let the marital songs be written, Let the
dirges disappear. Let the race of men now rise and take control.*

Margaret Abigail Walker

America has an obligation to world humanity in owning that it
suffers from a social cancer that is in dire need of healing. It is
the malady of racism that will always impede the progress America
is capable of, and will eventually be its downfall if there isn't a
moral cure in the offering. Past presidents have made pious public
statements about abandoning racism in America but littl has happened. We needed to take President Bush's statement on American
racial habits seriously when during his inaugural speech he urged us
to "abandon all the habits of racism." I have no doubt that the president said what he meant, however the American public needs more
than words that make us feel-good. Presidents can have the noble
intent about the perils of racism but without a plurality in moral
agreement and practice, it will not happen. It is pleasingly refreshing
to hear the words of "change, and freedom for all" from President
Barrack Obama. His words of hope come as the answer to a prayer
for a new long awaited day in America.

The first healing agent that is needed against racism is to recognize the need for reconciliation within the ranks of African and White Americans. The route to racial accord is to enter the sphere of public debate under the watchful direction of a skilled facilitator and openly discuss the struggles that America is confronted with because of its current racist practices. The U.S. Constitution is said to be the documented backbone of freedoms and desired practices; however, the American people need to enter a covenant relationship for the good of our continuing existence in the world order.

Until there is mutual respect between the races, reconciliation is impossible. The mutual respect begins in the social and economic arenas where African American people are recognized on equal par with their White counterparts. From a personal point of everyday experience, when I am in the company of a White majority, I feel that I must measure anything that I say for fear it will not be valued. That is not the case when White contributions are made. White people, for the most part, live secured lives of privilege, and make no apologies for their existence. Some of the feelings of perceived inadequacy by African American people must be overcome by their own sense of empowerment, and self worth.

During the 1950s and 60s a prescription for social healing was offered to America by an emphatic demonstration of nonviolent protest, which was led by the late Reverend Doctor Martin Luther King, Jr. The principal thesis of the civil rights movement, as articulated by King was, "we must live together as brothers and sisters, or perish together as fools." That statement was made to express the appreciation for the God given gift of life.

The annals of history provide a glimpse of how arrogance and greed contributed to the declination of the Roman Empire.[1] Rome, during the fifteenth year-CE, stood at the center as the foremost outpost of the empire. All roads led to Rome with her seven hills of imperial glory. The regal palace potentates ruled always in their favor with little regard for the proletariat. In many ways Rome proved to be a great melting pot of races, languages, cultures and ideas. There were many reasons for the decline of the Roman Empire. Each was related to the other. First, there was a decline in morals and values, public health problems, political corruption, and inflation, urban decay, increased military spending, and inferior technology. The empire was totally divided, and focused on problems that did not unify the nation. For a while the well trained Roman militia was able to fortify the Roman Empire by repelling the advances of the barbarians of Germany. The breakout of civil war in Italy caused a tactical mistake by reassigning the defending soldiers to join the fight in Italy. This move caused the Roman border to be vulnerable to attack, because there were no defending troops left for defense. After the overthrow of the last sitting emperor Augustulas Romulus in 509 **BC**, it is believed that the decline became a fact of Roman life, or what was left of it.

The review of Roman history parallels life in America, and gives cause for serious review of the times, and what equitable modifications should be taken in an effort to avoid the doom that is guaranteed if we continue the path we are on. If we are to remain the leader of the free world, we must give thought to the preservation of all human life, with no regard to race or culture. Respect for the good of human contributions, in building and maintaining a holistic social order, should be the ultimate goal of the American people.

The quest for unity and equality in America has been on the agenda of most people of goodwill, and many have joined the ranks of those who have made bold attempts to enlighten the general public to doing what is right and moral. It is no secret that persons who are vociferous and active about their august claims for freedom are oft times quieted with punitive action sanctioned by the ruling class. My cousin, Medgar Evers attempted to encourage African American Mississippians to register to vote, and he was cut down by Byron de la Beckwith, a White supremacist who waited for Evers to return to his home, and took his life by shooting him in the back with a 30 caliber bullet which mortally wounded him. His wife and children were watching a television broadcast of President John Kennedy about civil rights. Their viewing was interrupted by the sound of gunfire, and the discovery of Medgar on the floor of their carport gasping for his last breath. After 30 years and two deadlocked court decisions, Beckwith was found guilty of the crime.

James Earl Chaney, Michael Schwerner, and Andrew Goodman were murdered near Philadelphia, in Neshoba County, Mississippi.

Chaney, 21 (African American), Schwerner, 24 (White), and Goodman, 20 (White) had been working during the Mississippi Freedom Summer to register African Americans to vote. They were framed on trumped charges, arrested and released to the Klu Klux Klan, who beat and killed them. Vernon Dahmer, voting rights activist in the city of Hattisburg, Mississippi was firebombed by three carloads of Klansmen, because he made his place of business the place where African Americans could pay their poll tax.

Martin Luther King, Jr., tried to teach America how to live in unity, and because of his faith in God and love for humankind, his life was also snuffed out by an assassin. I was associated with King for approximately fourteen years from the Montgomery Bus Boycott to the Poor Peoples Campaign in Washington, D.C. He was a man with a social conscience, and a commitment to racial and cultural equality. I learned very early in our relationship that life is to be lived inclusive with others so that the cycle of learning and growing perpetuates itself. His yearning for human togetherness was his plight in his life. King was not limited to being the leader of African American people; instead he pricked the conscious and soul of diverse humanity and caused them to rethink their earthly purpose in human coexistence. He was an unusual man who did not come from a majority people but who came of the loins of a disinherited and disallowed people. His life has affected each of us in an indelible manner. Many Americans admonished King for his righteous teachings of love and obedience to the moral law, but because of his short witnessing presence, America will never be the same.

Throughout the existence of this great country, persons of good-will have been attempting to encourage it to live out its true meaning of brotherhood, and be the supreme example of what is right, according to the constitution and moral law. Among some of the different theatres of American social unrest and protest are slave abolition, women's suffrage, civil rights, minimum wage, campaigns for clean air and clean water, and the mobilization of groups to improve the social order and equitably improve the justice system. Before one can understand what is needed to heal America, there must be an understanding as to what the ills are. There have always been those who were of the persuasion that America is imperfect at best, and made attempts to identify areas where change was needed. The following campaigns were made manifest through the mediums of social movements that presented themselves as public nuisances to those who were non supportive of equitable coexistence:

- **Rosa Parks and the Montgomery Bus Boycott, 1955-56**
  Rosa Parks, an African American seamstress in Montgomery, Alabama sat down in the first seat behind the section reserved for white persons. Her unwillingness to move resulted in public demonstrations, which propelled the civil rights movement.

- **Desegregating Schools in Little Rock, Arkansas, 1957**
  By a decision of the Supreme Court, the school board of Little Rock, Arkansas voted to desegregate the public school system.

- **Sit-ins and freedom rides, 1960**
  The students of Greensboro, North Carolina, Nashville, Tennessee and Atlanta, Georgia began to sit-in at lunch counters to protest segregation. The success of the sit-ins gave impetus to the organization of the Student Nonviolent Coordinating Committee where the interstate bus freedom rides were organized and carried out.

- **The desegregation of Mississippi, 1962**
  Clyde Kennard attempted to enter the University of Southern Mississippi, and was jailed for seven years for being a racial agitator. James Meredith successfully sued for the admission to the University of Mississippi.

- **Birmingham, Alabama, 1963-1964**
  The civil rights movement directed its attention to the desegregation of Birmingham's merchants. The movement applied

various tactics, including sit-ins, marches for voting rights and committing to jail for civil disobedience
Infractions.

- **The March on Washington, 1963**
  In excess of 200,000 demonstrators positioned themselves in front of the Abraham Lincoln Memorial to address six major goals: integrated education, fair employment, increased federal works program, inclusive civil rights laws, safe and sanitary housing, and the passage of civil rights laws that protected African Americans.

These major campaigns and many more were directed at changing the status quo in the American system, because of the denial of basic human rights to those who were seen and regarded as lesser citizens. There has been, over the past four centuries, a hue and cry for America to live out the true meaning of fairness and togetherness by becoming one country, with the freedoms that we boast about afforded to all. Every social movement toward equality has been an effort to heal America of her wounds of human strife, and live out the true meaning of let freedom ring.

Since the civil rights movement of the 1960s, many of the churches, mosques, synagogues and other places of moral assembly have been silent on the systemic infractions against humanity. In the country's healing process, it is important to promote positive action from within the religious community where morality seems to be at the top of the agenda. Heretofore, we have depended on government and elected officials to cure our social ills, and while they can make responsible contributions, righteous institutions should be committed and dedicated to improving the quality of life of those who have been systematically omitted and disenfranchised. Another healing agent can be found at the voting booth, where political candidates are looking to the general public for support. In supporting the health of the country, we should send persons into public office who espouse equitable and moral ideals that are rooted in justice, mercy, righteousness and love for humanity. In sustaining good social health in America, it is important for corporate America to recognize the ordering of a level playing field in employment, marketing, retailing and service in efforts to supply goods and services. Because the American community has become increasingly more diverse, it is important to allay fears by community hosted dialogues on differences and the celebration of diversity. Building relationships is the most direct way to strengthen communities because we have more in common than we think. One America is the route to the fortification of our nation. In the poetic genius of Vine Victor Deloria, Jr., he wrote:

"Religion cannot be kept within the bounds of sermons and scriptures. It is a force in itself and calls for the integration of lands and peoples in harmonious unity. The lands [of the planet] wait for those who can discern their rhythms. The peculiar genius of each continent, each river valley, the rugged mountains, the placid lakes, all call for relief from the constant burden of exploitation."[2] The African American, Asian, Hispanic, African, European, Pacific Islander or any national who has made America home must work to make this a land of solidarity and peace.

There are countless incidents where exploitation has been a part of the lives of people who have no resemblance to the European culture but are every bit American as the people who exploit them. History records that the only authentic people who can rightfully claim their heritage to this land are the Native Americans, and they were exploited and violated by newcomers from Europe. With that piece of history realized, why can't we all get along? We will find comfort in those who are not like us, when we recognize the commonality in our humanness. The barriers that separate us are superficial at best, and need the secure hearts of those who understand strength in unity.

Most of our fears are ensconced in what we do not know, and the will to explore those fears is absent from our being. We often find ourselves suffering from paralysis of human diversity, when we deny ourselves an opportunity to expand. I remember when I was a student at Xavier University in New Orleans, Louisiana; racial segregation was the order of the time. One of the laws prohibited social race mixing in any form. Father Francis Berkley, a Catholic priest served as the music director at Saint Patrick's Catholic

Church, which was located in a commercial district. There was a need for a regular liturgical choir to serve the different Masses. Father Berkeley sought to build such a choir of vocal music students from the local African American, and white universities, (Loyola, Tulane, Newcomb College, Xavier, Dillard). The liturgical choir was made up of white students from Loyola, Tulane, and Newcomb, and African American students from Xavier and Dillard. This was my first racial integrated experience. We were actually breaking the law, because, often we socialized with wine and cheese after rehearsals. This was Father Berkley's early contribution to bridging the racial divide.

CHAPTER IV

A NEW BEGINNING

****

I'd like to get away from earth awhile and then come back to it and begin over. May no fate willfully misunderstand me, and half grant what I wish and snatch me away not to return. Earth's the right place for love: I don't know where it's likely to go better.

Robert Frost

We have come to a time of the great awakening from a deep slumber of inertia, which has rendered more confusion than the corporate ability to peacefully coexist in supporting human relationships. From time to time we are bound to take an introspective look into our lives to determine whether we measure up to the standards of a good neighbor to those in whom we find comfort, or to those we hardly know. We live in some American communities that are culturally and racially diverse with different beliefs, languages, philosophical thought, attitudes and behaviors. They demonstrate no curiosity as to the make up of the totality of the community. No matter who we are or what we adhere to, we are all in the same boat. Bernard Baruch, an American financier and Statesperson, said it well in his statement: "We didn't all come over on the same ship, but we're all in the same boat."[1] Unfortunately, we are compacted together without the knowledge of our given differences or commonalities. Therefore, we are left with the freedom to speculate about one another with no prior information or background that could be helpful in determining our likenesses. We are left with making judgments in a stereotypical manner.

Having lived in three markedly divided southern cities beginning in Jackson, Mississippi, and on to New Orleans, Louisiana and Montgomery, Alabama, I am a product of societal separation with definitive laws that were enacted to keep the African American and White races apart. I distinctly remember playing with White children until the age of twelve years old, and their parents abruptly ended our socialization, because of the teachings and laws that prohibited further fraternization. As innocent children, we struggled with the parental wisdom of interrupting our social development. If we, in our innocence, could have had a role in the architecture of our development, the world would be far different, and without the social divide. The root cause of the chasm that separates us is found in our inability and unwillingness to breach the wall of fear, as we fear what we do not know.

After sharing the American environment for approximately four hundred years, and missing our true greatness, we are led to examine the results of our introspectiveness and enter a phase of a new beginning. What directions have we gone that were right, or those that were wrong? What have we learned that we might modify for a better society? New beginnings come with a dared behavior to risk the unknown with faith in expecting the right return. It means venturing to engage non- traditional relationships in an effort to strengthen the immediate social order; also, exercising untouched curiosity about people and communities, who are unlike us, and finding ways to enter into informative, respectful, and reasonable dialogue. Institutions that make up the community of faith are natural venues for such gatherings, as are other places of public diverse assembly.

While our past has been sordid with greed, ignorance, and violence, I have witnessed, in the twenty-first century, a positive promise in the American people, and their willingness to embark on a new beginning. While that aspect of our lives is not celebrated in blatant ways, signs of a fresh approach are evident. It is a quiet developing movement that we should all join for the betterment of our beloved country. New beginnings commence with self. There is much to be done in changing the face of America and the negative inner feelings of our citizens. In an introspective review each individual can take stock of self and make improvements in interpersonal relationships with those whom we have bypassed, because of stereotypical prejudgments.

We have been guilty of institutional racism and discrimination, which has contributed to character assassination, and in some cases moral decline. Corporate America has an obligation to support unity among the people it serves. Leading corporate organizations across America have come to understand market place diversity where they are involved in business, and have realized profits in their practice. They have come to recognize increasing multicultural, multifaceted, and multilingual entities throughout commodity users and suppliers. Not only is it a reality in the changing demographics but also it is also good business. Therefore, it is not a surprise that businesses that are more profitable, and taking a leadership role in their communities have come to capitalize in the practice of diversity. The Institute For Corporate Diversity is an exhaustive compilation of companies who are at the cutting edge of diversity.[2] Not only is the practice of diversity good for America, it is making a difference in the global community as well. Taking advantage of diversity is a large part of the new beginning.

The American educational system has an emphatic place in shaping and nurturing the minds of our students. Teachers wield much influence in the developmental process of young inquisitive learners. In years past, I recall explaining to my parents that what the teacher taught or said was the last word, even after parental pronouncement. Institutions of learning are meant to lead and guide the thinking process and deductive process. Where is there a better venue than school to structure the response to the problematic future? We are living in an age where knowledge is the key to survival, if we lose the battle of conquering the unknown, we have ceased our purpose for being, and we squander the pregnant idea of educational enhancement. In the eminent words of the great nineteenth century French poet, Victor Hugo, "Greater than the tread we face them together with a new beginning of mighty armies, is an idea whose time has come."[3] Education must take its prominent place in the new beginning.

Much has been said of the community of faith in its leadership role of upholding the tenants of righteousness, mercy, justice and love. Today is the time a sermon should be seen instead of heard. The churches, synagogues, mosques, and other places of religious assembly have grown in bricks and mortar, but there appears to be stagnation in the growth of those who have dedicated themselves to spiritual development. No other acts of care giving have been practiced as much as in the early Christian church. The reading of the Acts of the Apostles, Chapter 2:44-45 provides an accounting of the depth of living in community. Here we learn what Jesus meant by, "In as much as you have done it unto one of the least of these my brothers, you have done it unto me." There is no greater joy in life than belonging to a sharing community. Down through the path of human history, it has been iterated by "united we stand, divided we fall." Abraham Lincoln in this analogy attempted to solidify the American community in his love to preserve the union. When the old has been tried and failed, new beginnings become necessary as long as there is hope. Where there is human will, impossibilities are not a consideration in mounting the challenges ahead.

Our nation experienced the horrible years of the dehumanization of Native; and African Americans. Some of the ill - willed behaviors caused the nation to enter into an unjust civil war been that further divided the country. We allowed our wills to fall prey to this ter-rible war, where 618,000...lives were lost to the host of death. We weathered the ravages of this senseless war by bringing the nation together beneath one flag. The Great Depression of 1929 saw the nation lose its economic footing. Cities around the world suffered serious economic downfalls, the collapse of the stock market, unem-ployment, soup lines, housing shortages, and over indebtedness and deflation. Even through this dark period of American life, we dem-onstrated the will and resilience to persevere with a new beginning. It was difficult but we did it. In times of great devastation, this great country rose up from the ashes of bleakness to assume its rightful leadership role in the global community.

I have no doubt about America's ability to persevere through times of great difficulty, because the will to work hard enough toward recovery is on our side. Our strength is found in Irving Berlin's song, "God Bless America." It is a patriotic song that embodies the very soul of America when times are uncertain. We have the where-with-all to overcome perilous times when we face them together with a new beginning.

Pronounced freedom for African Americans became a reality, in writing, one hundred forty-five years ago. Throughout the annals of time, there was always a period of starting over again in the attempt to overcome the perils and devastations of the past. Endurance, under girded by hope in a better day, has sustained the lifelong pilgrimage of African Americans from slavery to the twenty-first century. Life has been fraught with disappointments, rejections, and false accusations, but it has taken an undying faith to pierce the veil of "never" to override fear and to believe we will eventually prevail and achieve the obtainable. The new beginning for uncompromised justice is upon us, and the time is now. Now is the time, as opportunities have come to those who have been the disavowed and disallowed victims of the America that has brought us global shame. Only God of the universe can respond as to why it has taken so very long to assume a new beginning. It was the artfully crafted words of Martin Luther King, Jr. "...however difficult the moment, however frustrating the hour, it will not be long, because "truth crushed to earth will rise again... How long? Not long, because the arc of the moral universe is long, but it bends toward justice." I am convinced that America is at that point of a new beginning, and the rising sun of a new time shines its beams over the plains of our beloved land. An idea whose time has come in the person of Barack Hussein Obama, the first African American President of the United States of America. While many other firsts African American, and other minority cultures are on the horizon to fill other high profile offices, America is moving forward in spite of the naysayers who believe, to be American, you must be blond, blue eyed, and skin free from color. As we experience more interaction with global nations, we come to realize the world is occupied with diversity sharing what the earth has to offer. Education and expanded travel have been influences in the recognition of the need to expand our relational thinking beyond those who resemble us. Time has revealed that change is inevitable, and new ways can be taught, experienced, and learned in societal improvement.

African Americans have continued to improve their socio-economic condition in significant ways since the Civil Rights Movement of the 1960s. We have witnessed an expanding African American economic growth across the United States. The desire and advantage of accessing higher education has been exceptionally evident in the availability of higher grades of employment in government and the private sector. However, due to the historic social cancer of racial prejudice there continue to be vestiges of discrimination and segregation. With understanding, and effort it appears that we are experiencing positive signs toward better relations. We are experiencing a new beginning, because many people in all races and cultures are working at it.

Of all of the minority groups in America, African Americans have become most increasingly involved in positions of power. The high number of Congressional Delegates, and big city mayors gives evidence for this forward movement. Progress is especially recognized in the area of economics. In 2004, African Americans maintained the second-highest median earnings of minority groups. It is a well-known fact that the talk show hostess Oprah Winfrey was the wealthiest African American of the twentieth century. Her overall wealth was reported in the year 2010 as 2.7 billion dollars. This is quite significant, as we reflect on slavery ending over one hundred forty-five years ago. More can be written about the wealth of African American athletes, entertainers, and business ventures. Historically, we have learned more about great African American contributions to the human fabric of America. Such names as Jan Matzeliger, who created a machine to mass- produce shoes, Elijah McCoy, who invented the lubricating system for steam engines, Garrett A. Morgan introduced us to the gas mask, and traffic signal, and Dr. Daniel Hale Williams, paved the way for endless successful open heart surgeries, one of which was done for the author. These names are a few among many who laid the foundation for useful implements that are currently used in the world.

Now we enter a new generation of African Americans in the 21st century who have no knowledge of slavery or the days of 19th century Jim Crow practices. They believe they are entitled to all of the rights of this land of freedom, as is every citizen. They have learned well what their rights are, and many are willing to invest their time and talents in a system that hopefully will deliver their entitlements. We have come too far to go back to the days of fear, defeat, and doubt. Over the past four hundred years, African Americans have learned their lessons of survival and achievement well.

We come now to a new era of exploration and further development that has more to do with assuming a true partnership to advance the perceived goals of building a stronger and more unified America. We are slowly moving into a sphere of understanding that to succeed, we must come to recognize, respect, and appreciate what each contributes, regardless of origin, color, ancestry or culture. America will survive because of its perceived strength, and leadership in the world community. The new beginning is ushered in with the unabashed celebration of unity among American men and women of all races and cultures. It is this kind of change where the focus of true community living is directed to equitable human coexistence, and where a balanced cooperative effort in enhancing the beloved community.

It is clearly defined and proved that the ways in which Americans have lived divided in their respected enclaves have yielded dissension, alienation, and stereotyping. As we take stock on what does not work, we have the opportunity to reshape our values, and those tenets that take us closer to an ordered, and relational society. The new beginning is changing from the old, and taking on the new where everyone has a chance to succeed.

CHAPTER V

A NEW LOOK IN CHANGING TIMES

****

*At some future period, the civilized races of man
will almost certainly exterminate and replace the
savage races throughout the world.*

Charles Darwin

In the human experience, change is inevitable, either sameness will become a bore or someone will present a different idea and usher in something new. No world dynasty has gone on forever, because flourishing new thoughts and needs become the change agents of the time. When our forefathers authored the U.S. Constitution, The Declaration of Independence, and the Bill of Rights, there was no way to grasp the understanding and appreciation for these laws in future generations. They were written to encompass the population that existed during the time they were crafted. The question is often raised about what Thomas Jefferson's true meaning was in the Declaration when he wrote, "We hold these truths to be self-evident, that all men are created equal..." Could he have meant that African Americans were also included? In as much as slavery was very much a way of life during the eighteenth century, it is difficult to make the case that the language included African Americans. However, we as soldiers and defenders of civil rights, during the marching years of the 1960s, held on to the written legal documents that sealed America, and attempted to make manifest those carefully crafted words that we assumed included all men of this free land.

In my opening statement of this chapter, the point is made that change is inevitable, and it shall always be. No order or institution remains forever. Edward Gibbon's treatise, "The Decline and Fall of the Roman Empire," is a detailed account of what human greed and corruption can do and did to a nation. In spite of the not so good times for the disallowed and disavowed in America, those who are open to a better way of living, and take advantage of the opportunities offered, have faired and succeeded because of positive change.

This change comes and is accepted because of human commonalities. It is not unrealistic for a person of privilege to assume the sufferings of others who are not as privileged. That was the greatness of love for fellow persons when many White persons of goodwill left the comfort of their surroundings and joined the great liberating army of the poor and destitute to bring attention to their plight. Not only did many of our White brothers and sisters share ranks in the lines of civil rights marches, they also gave their lives as the ultimate for change.

America has now witnessed the inevitability of change with the overwhelming election of our forty-fourth president, Barack Obama. He comes with a reformist message of change and hope for an exciting future. He is the first person of color to ascend to the White House, and the symbol of this presidency speaks to a time that an idea has come. This is a time that I assumed that I would not personally witness. I am a true believer in Divine Order, and the election of Obama is cast in that belief.

Historians have recorded that men and women were destined by Divinity to assume a certain role in their lives. From these historical accounts, it seems that whenever we find ourselves in times of great peril or devastation, God lifts up a prophet or prophetess from our ranks to lead us with His message of repentance and salvation.

Change comes through great leaders, who are often rare. Often men and women will lay claim to that title, but then no one follows them. Some people are elected or appointed to leadership positions, but then they falter or fail to act. Others abuse their powers to satisfy their massive egos. But without faithful, ethical, and moral leaders, people wander from truth. America has wandered for over four hundred years through the good and not so good times. Somehow, in spite of ourselves, we have been protected by a power that we sometimes ignore. I believe we are standing at the gates of a change that we need.

The truth became known when the good people of Iowa heard God's plea through Barack Obama, and they rose up like eagles, and soared to the White House with him to bring our beloved country to peaceful coexistence. Many Americans celebrate the advent of a new and changed America with great anticipation of what Mr. Obama has promised in leading an inclusive country, and we have every right to experience the hope of liberation from the past politics that enslaved us, and made us wards of the wealthy and elite. The world rejoiced because of a phenomenal race and victorious presidential election. He has ignited renewed trust and faith in the America we hail and love. The election of this exciting and youthful president has given our country a hope that has been lost in the rubbles of greed and power. Never shall we forget that there are those who profited by the anguish and labors of those who do not enjoy privilege, and those who have miles to go before they realize promised change. Positive change will come when the American people experience change in their hearts. It will not come with the changing of the president. A new guard can dream of a new and more equitable order, but it takes the troops to realize the dream.

A case in point, immediately after President Obama was elected, racist graffiti was evidenced on the campus of North Carolina, and Appalachian State Universities. Students at the Christian Baylor University were a state of unrest; an African American woman over-heard some white male students talking about how they were going to beat up any black student who walked by. It has been further reported that someone hung a noose on Baylor's campus and burned Obama political signs. White and African Americans of good will are going to be the determinants of an America that will rise from the ashes of hatred and violence to a new day of hope and unity.

Change is not limited to a new and unusual president; it is found in the spirits of people who are weary of the struggles of resentment, discord, and rejection. The time has come to experience the renaissance of a new day where we all work together to eradicate fear, and bring respect to ordinary living. For two hundred years black African slaves used their spiritual imagination to see over the horizon in interpreting their songs. These songs became symbols of great hope for freedom. When they sang, "Ah'm so glad dat trouble don lass always," they psychologically projected themselves into a new day without the troubles of the time.

As generations come and go, new ideas replace the old, and much of history is forgotten, however, we need to study history to avoid those thing that cause repeated mistakes. While the world progresses, it is important to place education at the top of life's agenda. Technological and scientific development is what propels the world order, and we must be prepared to operate in such an advanced environment. There are, and have been many concerns and questions about equal education for our students. Educators must be aware of the academic deficiencies in many minority schools, as well as the different learning styles of students from various cultures. It is because of this lack of knowledge we have developed modern methods of study and testing, without being armed with basic knowledge of the differences in races and cultures.. It is with this lack of knowledge, and educational readiness that many minority students find themselves lagging in scholarship. African Americans and other minority cultures are not represented in appreciable numbers in schools of higher education that are traditionally White.

The time has come for real change in increased leadership development training for all historically African American colleges and universities. In the recognition of world change, we must give attention to nontraditional issues that matter in promoting a unified planet. These United States have an opportunity to wave the baton of positive change. We must insist that the old American order of politics change to reflect a disciplined, and a more respectful breed of political aspirants who will address the will of the people. This gives reasons as to why our educational system must be inclusive to meet the changing world.

Education must be a global priority agenda item. Military arms have been the focal point for many nations who labor under the aegis of fear of destruction instead of prioritizing education, and broader human relations. There comes a point in time when we as the global community must subdue the implements of war and move the education agenda forward toward a more enlightened world. In these changing times America would be well advised to invest in the future through a more concentrated emphasis on the education of our youth. In a nation of wealth and state of the art resources, America's youth are lagging behind many other nations in the sciences and mathematics. In a Washington Post article, dated December 5, 2007, page AD7, Maria Glod wrote, "The disappointing performance of U.S. teenagers in math and science on an international exam…has sparked calls for improvement in public schools to help the country keep pace in the global economy." She further stated that, "U.S. students were further behind in math, trailing counterparts in 23 countries. It seems that our priorities are out of order, and need to be realigned to meet the competing world. All of this has to do with the new direction in which the world is headed in keen competition on all fronts. What if we overcome the enemy, and haven't the skills to maintain an ordered society?"

The problem with education and these changing times is complex but not insolvable. It appears the approach to good education is to construct a community comprehensive sphere of learning, which points to better academically prepared teachers, trained parents, prepared civic leaders, the community of faith, and a balanced program of study and preparation. It is paramount that well prepared teachers are attracted to the profession by reasonable salaries and benefits. This approach would be a wise community investment for a secured future. Changing times mean to reorder old approaches, forgetting political expediencies, greed, vanity, personal gratification, and using the local school boards as a step to greater politics.

America will not and cannot go forward until we come to accept that we are a major factor in the geometry of global change, and our views of life in the future must conform to the greater cause of survival in regarding all points of view, whether we agree or not.

CHAPTER VI

AN IDEA WHO'S TIME HAS COME

****

The vitality of thought is in adventure. Ideas won't keep. Something must be done about them. When the idea is new, it's custodians have fervor, Live for it, and, if need be die for it.

Alfred North Whitehead

Ideas are formed in thought that comes by the mind. They also rise to levels of actual concepts when we speak of people or places, and have much to do with the ability of reasoning. There comes a time when change is the order of the moment. It is a time when relevant ideas reach the stage of maturation, and are pregnant with the freshness and newness of life's expectations. An infant enters the scene of ongoing life with a mind of its own. Accommodations are made to provide comfort to a budding new life, and we strive to create an atmosphere that will serve as an incubator for positive growth and development. Sometimes, in our selfishness, we offer impediments that blunt and stifle progress to the extent that we remain the status quo. The most detrimental blow to humanity is to stifle an idea whose time has come, which will flourish and bring benefit to all who await progress.

Sometimes new ideas appear to threaten the status quo and render it obsolete. Progress is not possible without improvements of what has been tried and used. Our lives are for- ever changing, because of the evolution of our environment, and the, never ending, search for new expedient ways to improve upon what is, to what can be. In many expressions of life, there are beliefs that a fresh new approach to living can fill the void of a battered existence. Many persons have made such a change, because of the recognition of the faith perspective. In exploring faith perspectives, we find the much talked about Islam faith on a fast track spreading over the world. This idea of faith is founded in one's will to surrender to the only true Islamic god, Allah, who Moalems proclaim is worthy of worship. Hinduism is the one true culture of Indians in India. Siddhartha Gautama founded Buddhism in the sixth century. The history of Judaism has been identified as the oldest known religion extending far back as 4000 years ago, Chrisrianity has served the Western hemisphere for centuries, and many more religions of the world. Unlike most religions, during it's ancient beginning, it rested on the belief of one God who promised the coming of the Messiah in unknown days to come. The coming of the Messiah to the Jews was an expected deliverer from a life fraught with pain, prejudice, and death. The idea of this deliverer was to usher in a new day of freedom. These various faith journeys, of old, have served as a panacea of the ills of life, and mankind has always placed confidence in an unseen power, which is found in hope.

Over the past four hundred years, America has looked to a higher order, in the name of God, to guide us through perilous times. During the time of the American Civil War, Secretary of the Treasury Salmon P. Chase was confronted with multiple requests from American Christians to place the name of God on coins used by the United States, However, that which received the most attention was a letter to Secretary Chase from Reverend M. R, Watkinson, of Township, Pennsylvania.[1] From this discourse, the nations motto, "In God We Trust," was placed on U.S. coinage. America has existed under this very powerful idea, which became the motto of the United States of America.

In the heat of the vicissitudes in the continuation of the forming and development of America, the motto still stands as a reminder that our trust is in God. While much of the political, economic, and social disorder recently has been unsteady, we continue to maintain our faith in God. His name was elevated during the Civil War, during times of great distress, as in the Great Depression, and especially during the American Civil Rights Movement where this initiative was founded on the very principles of God's teachings. This was a time of meaningful teaching and learning in America, as the Civil Rights movement had no money, no influence with power, no power brokers, and no kept promises. Reliance was in the wealth of faith and hope, which won the hearts and support of many persons who were transformed from evil to good. America underwent partial social transformation from the legislative halls to the behavior of the general public. It was a time of reformation and transition from a buried idea to resurrection. This was possible because freedom for African Americans was an idea whose time had come. It came during perilous times when righteous practices had long been denied, and discounted, and it was a time when the very motto of America became meaningful and took on the righteous intent.

Historians have recounted times when great awareness and cure have come at unexpected moments in history, when evil was transformed to good. Ideas are synonymous with change, and when conditions are in need of improvement or need to move in a new direction, the time for something different or a change becomes evident. New ideas are born out of fatigue with the old and tried ventures that have not succeeded. So long as there is life upon this planet, change remains inevitable, and new ideas will come forth.

Stories are in abundance where life and human behavior have been positively altered, because someone was driven to the outer limits by an untried idea. The fields of art, medicine, science, technology, law, education, and many others have advanced to far greater heights, because someone(s) dared the outer limits.

Dr. Benjamin Carson, the director of pediatric neurosurgery at Johns Hopkins Hospital in Baltimore, Md. is a young African American man who by earthly accounts was far outside of the arena of any kind of success due him.[2] He was a young man growing up in one of Detroit, Michigan's racially segregated neighborhoods, raised by a single mother, abandoned by an absentee father, he had negative behavioral traits, and was prone for trouble. His bio reports that it took the courage and love of his mother, Sonya Copeland

Carson, who dropped out of school in the third grade, to instill in him and his brother, Curtis, the value of education.

After an early marriage at thirteen years old, two boy children were born to Sonya and her husband, Robert Solomon. The marriage ended in divorce, when Dr. Carson was eight years old. He was at the bottom of his class, as his classmates referred to him as "dummy." In his mother's determination, she insisted that her boys would improve their grades, she denied them television watching, and reduced their outdoors play until they had completed their homework assignments. She also required them to read two library books a week, and to provide her written reports, despite her limited education. The boys discovered, after this ordeal was over, that their mother could not read.

Today, Dr. Carson is a leading pioneer surgeon, and made history in 1987 by performing surgery to separate a pair of Siamese twins. Such surgical procedures up to this point had always failed. The twins were separated successfully and are now living their lives.

There are countless contributions, in the form of great ideas that have come from the minds of African Americans who dreamed of better ways to enhance our lives. The blood bank was an idea of Dr. Charles Richard Drew. He recognized the need for blood preservation over a period of time. Drew was a revolutionist in the medical profession, which to his credit saved many lives. There are other inventive ideas that were introduced, patented, and marketed, such as Garrett Augustus Morgan's invention of the stoplight. Early in the 20th century, the roads were overcome with horse drawn wagons, cycles, and newly built motor powered vehicles, as well as with people. In the absence of rules for the road, Morgan witnessed many accidents, thereby giving rise to his idea of the stoplight. In 1902 Willis Haviland Carrier invented, patented, and introduced the first air conditioning machine. Edwin Howard Armstrong is known for inventing FM radio in 1933. Among women with practical ideas, Josephine Cochran designed the first dishwasher. In August 1913. Tabitha Babbitt is heralded with the ingenious idea of inventing the circular saw that lessened the strokes of the two-man pit saw.

Good and practical ideas change societies in which people live, that they may reap their full entitlements to what they are offered.

Victor Hugo, the French poet, playwright and human rights activist among many other interests, wrote of an idea in such a powerful way. "An invasion of armies can be resisted, but not an idea whose time has come." The infamous diabolical ideas and behavior of Adolph Hitle destroyed many lives and brought doom to many innocent people. Ideas are not always for the good existent life.

For the Christian, the advent of Jesus Christ was God's idea of a fresh renewal of the world order, and a demonstrative lesson on how we should live in positive relationships with one another. I hasten to state that other faith perspectives follow the same rule, but under different inspiration, directions, and guidelines. The God given gift of the mind is God's creative expression to perpetuate the ongoing development of the world order. America has always been a nation of countless ideas that have contributed to her greatness

Philosophically, innate ideas exist in a sphere unconnected or well defined from life, as we know it. Usually it is also a belief that ideas are derived from personal experiences. Plato, in earlier philosophical accounts, held that "ideas are perfect, external, and unchallengeable, and that knowledge of material things is not really knowledge; real knowledge can only be had of unchanging ideas." Rene Descartes thoughts of ideas were like images of things, and it was to these alone that he thought the name idea: belonged. John Locke, in contrast to Plato's understanding of "idea" was whatsoever the object of the understanding when a man thinks. David Hume differs from Locke by reducing "idea" to perception, which in the final process are impressions.

The aforementioned philosophers expressed their differences regarding "ideas;" however in the final analysis, there is agreement that ideas are cognitives which can be stimulated by a pressing moment fueled by past events, impressions, personal experiences or the need to resolve an immediate concern.

As the world turns, we are constantly confronted with changing times and the accompanying problems therein. Somehow we are driven to overcome our perils, either by circumstance or by some unusual personality with great ideas to spearhead a new, and more advanced path to improvement. Men and women are equipped to realize ideas that have never been tried before, and the world has been better for such ventures. In 1796, the English physician, Edward Jenner took a chance with an idea he had about a cure for the dreadful smallpox disease.[143] He followed up on a folklore that said that dairymaids who were found with cowpox were immune to smallpox. In his search for a cure, he inoculated an eight-year-old boy with smallpox vaccin by inserting pus in his veins extracted from a woman with cowpox. With this experiment, Dr. Jenner proved that having cowpox provided immunization against smallpox. Because of Dr. Jenner's idea and eventual experiment; smallpox has been abated all over the world, unfortunately some nations of ill will have entertained the possibility of unleashing the smallpox germ for germ warfare. germ warfare.

The art of creative thinking should be a welcome addition to positive world development, while continuous improvement of high technology provides a network of connectors for easy exchange of new ideas. As a result the world becomes smaller, and people come closer together for advanced change. Positive change is a matter of choice, and the value one places on "tomorrow." If we make wise investments today in order to reap greater dividends in the future we have done a good and wise thing. Unless our laudable dreams and ideas are converted into action, we have nothing ventured, and nothing gained. Good and positive ideas are a daily activity of the mind, it is when we are dormant about possibilities that life becomes inactive, and no benefit is realized.

When an idea is born, the time has come to nurture it toward concrete action for a greater benefit for the whole of humanity. It begins with you. In the words of Henry David Thoreau, "If a man is not in step with his companions, perhaps it's because he hears a different drummer. Let him step to the music he hears, no matter how measured or far away." Every one has their purpose for living.

CHAPTER VII

THE OLIVE BRANCH CONCEPT

****

Sadly I walk'd within the field, to see what comfort it would yield;
And as I went my private way. An olive-branch before me lay;
And seeing it, I made a stay, and took it up, and view'd it; then
Kissing the omen, said Amen; Be, be it so, and let this be
A divination unto me; That in short time my woes shall cease,
And love shall crown my end with peace.

Robert Herrick

We have slighted those things that bring us closer together by reordering natural human relationships. Our basic common nature yearns for peace, while we seek it by all means, including some ways that are not understandable, and are destructive. We call implements of violence peacemakers that are used to bring about the absence of turmoil, even though they may also bring about an end to life. Disagreements are often settled by war and strife, and when the fighting is over, we gravitate to the table of peace. This has been the pattern of existence since the beginning of man. Sometimes symbols provide great and memorable meanings in the makeup of our lives, and the offering of the olive branch has come to represent the need for peace where there has been discord, unreasonable thinking, and the threat of violence. I have never understood why the olive branch is not offered at the onset of conflict. However, I have come to believe it is in man's DNA to defend his position by putting the adversary in a defenseless state, which constitutes division.

Oft times division is preceded by poor communication, and the unwillingness to examine the breach in order to further progress in relationships. Poor communication is usually at the heart of any mis-understanding, and is relatively properly resolved in an atmosphere of goodwill, and by changing places with the other side of the issue. The most potent force for good or evil is communication. Ayal Hurst writes about four basic styles of communication[1].

- **Aggressive** - These personalities come on too strong and their energy bombards or pushes people,
- **Passive** – Passive communicators tend to appear weak and self - conscious.
- **Passive Aggressive** – They will say one thing to your face and another behind your back, and
- **Assertive** – Their communications are compassionate in their delivery. It is the ability to relay a clear message without blaming. The Assertive style comes close to offering the olive branch for improving dialogue in problem solving.

Communication is awareness of your own inner being, and how you relate to others for a growing experience. It is a good feeling to be secure in your knowledge of a discussed subject, but it is good to be respectful in hearing another view of that subject, which could add knowledge to what you already know.

It is better to have even exchanges in communication than to reach a point of total disagreement, or division, about something that can appeal to sound reasoning. However, it is always beneficial to identify a common denominator of mutual understanding for an amicable resolve. Such understanding makes way for an offering of an olive branch, which is the philosophical beginning of under-standing, peace and unity. There is a memorable story found in the book of Genesis that recounts a time of strife between Abram and Lot's herdsmen. Because they both had too many cattle to graze on their land, conflict arose between their herdsmen. Abram, the wiser of the two, offered what might be understood in today's language as an olive branch. He said, "Let there be no strife between you and me, and between our herdsmen, because we are brothers. We can separate our herds, and you can occupy any section of the land that you desire." Lot, selfishly, took for himself the more fertile land, and parted. Abram saw the wisdom in maintaining peace between the two factions where all could survive and save harmony. This is an example of creatively finding ways to live and thrive together.

Because we are created distinctively different, freedom of diverse thoughts and expressions is greatly encouraged with respect to differences. It is advantageous to the total process when we blend our contributions to a common end where all will benefit. The stalemate of rigid divisions hinders progress causing greater conflict in the process.

In his quotation of division, Sir Thomas Browne, 1605 – 1682, English author, wrote:

"I could never divide myself from any man upon the difference of opinion, or be angry with his judgment for not agreeing with me in that from which perhaps within a few days I should dissent myself." It is obvious that Sir Thomas Browne favored the flow of progress as opposed to the status quo, and where he saw himself stymieing the process he would absent himself.

Americans have come to recognize a new era of culturally diverse immigrant inhabitants who understand that their rights should not be abridged, and are entitled to all that our country has to offer. We have existed under a divided system for such a period of time that it is difficult for some of our citizens to adapt to a changed way of living with others. Those of us who are outside of favorable opportunities, who have been disavowed, and disallowed, are creating public tension that beckons the attention of those in the ruling class. This social divide necessitates a peaceful bridge that will usher in harmonious relationships, but not without the accoutrements that provide for all a fair and equitable chance at making life work in the balance.

The balance of peace hangs on the willingness and desire that people demonstrate in closing the socio/economic gap that separates us from being all we can be in a society of bounty and promise. The olive branch, to be offered, is found in the will of those who understand and embrace harmony in a configuration of the disquieted masses. Peace and understanding come at a price of forgiveness, and acceptance of forgiveness. It is the willingness to risk criticism from a third party which has having little understanding about the conflicting issue(s) involved. It also takes into account just how valuable the connection is between the opposing contestants. In an attempt to settle any dispute that ruptures a meaningful relationship, it is reasonable for one of the parties to consider offering an olive branch with the intent of establishing good faith.

In human imperfections, we often venture into matters for our own self -interest, and we will defend our coveted position at a cost that is sometimes difficult to compromise. We want what makes sense for our own gain. There comes a time when something has to give for a bigger gain, and we should be open to the art of bringing a peaceful resolution to the disagreement. Because we are opinionated we differ from time to time, which in many cases results in conflicting views, and thereby dividing us Conflict is normal and healthy, because if there is no conflict, we will never know if we have arrived at the very best solution to a problem. God made us individuals with different minds, and there comes a time when we are bound to disagree. Show me any set of individuals who are in constant agreement on everything, and I will show you a failed relationship. Divisions in relationships are realized whenever people disagree with ideas, thoughts, expressions, motivations propelled by others, and actions taken in the absence of consensus.

In working with others, it is vitally important to be in touch with your own feelings and emotions, your strengths and weaknesses, and your ability to give a fair ear to ideas that are not your own. Within group dynamics divisions can destroy any worthwhile venture that has the possibility of benefiting the needs of many persons who are not accounted for in the deliberations. This is exactly what often happens in our national legislative debates. There should always be an availing opportunity to resort to a healthy process for resolving differences that divide us. The Olive Branch Concept is always a good way to break a stalemate, however, there are other ways to approach agreement:

- The ability to be open to differing points of view;

- The will to forgive others who differ with your ideas;

- The desire to participate in compromises where possible; and

- The willingness to accept a supporting resolution that will satisfy all parties.

Most individuals struggle with giving ear and listening to another point of view, while they pose themselves to advance their point of view, thereby missing some factors that could be beneficial in the outcome. Listening respectfully adds an important dimension of respect to all who are involved in resolving the subject matter. It is another reminder of the Golden Rule, "Do unto others as you would have them do unto you."

In overcoming the different divides in our lives that rob us of the fullness of the precious gift of life, we should exhaust every opportunity employ the Olive Branch approach, and search out those attributes that positively enhance us as the human family of God where there is always peace, and tranquility.

CHAPTER VIII

HOPE BEYOND THE HORIZON

****

*Let us contemplate our forefathers, and posterity, and resolve
to maintain the rights bequeathed us from the former, f
or the sake of the latter. The necessity of the times,
more than ever, calls for our utmost circumspection,
deliberation, fortitude and perseverance. Let us remember
that "if we suffer tamely a lawless attack upon our liberty,
we encourage it, and involve others in our doom."
It is a very serious consideration...that millions yet unborn
may be the miserable sharers of the event.*

Samuel Adams

It is widely believed that hope produces successful results in the lives of those who practice, and live with faith. Hope is the outlook that what is desired will be obtained to the satisfaction of the hopeful. In the theological context, hope is considered along with faith and love. It very likely that hope renders good to the faithful in any context in which it comes.

The nineteenth century poet, Robert Browning, once wrote, "Ah, but a man's reach should exceed his grasp or what's a heaven for." Browning, in his stretch for what may have seemed to be impossible, was realistic in testing his innate power to obtain the unreachable. Man has the ability to move beyond his immediate realm of existence by exercising the faith perspective. We can conquer that which has never before been conquered when we are put to the test. Even in cases of death, I have read accounts of brief death experiences where the resuscitation of life was a major factor in prolonging the life experience. Self written stories have been recorded where persons have been medically pronounced dead, however, they were conscience of their after being. They wrote of a short journey through a tunnel, and the end was a bright light so bright that looking into it was, somewhat difficult. The peace and calmness they experienced was inviting, causing them to want not to return to their earthly life. Many accounts have reported this same experience, There is hope for the strong, and purposeful minded.

The United States of America has been on a downward path in morality, values, respect, governance, people relations, religion, politics, corruption, youth development, economics, healthcare, and the overall social order. We have come to the time when hope is all we can depend on. Hope finds itself at the core of deep and abiding faith in God in all His sovereignty. This hope is what fueled perseverance in the souls of black slaves during perilous times in their lives which appeared to be hopeless. This is the same hope that returned many of our war torn U.S. armed forces back to American soil, after having been involved in bloody wars in far away lands. Hope keeps dysfunctional families together in harmony, when it seems all is lost. It also transforms an illicit drug using family member to a normal productive contributing human being. It is better to live in hope and great expectation than drown in cautious defeat.

We have now come to the test of time, and the dividends of our many years of investing in hope. On January 20, 2009, an African American by the name of Barack Hussein Obama was inaugurated as America's forty-fourth President of these United States. Because of the deep attitudes of rejection and hatred for African Americans, I resigned to accept that never would I experience a time such as this. Positive change is being experienced in America, and while we still have a long way to go, enough people of good will have acted responsibly. Unlike those before him, President Obama's pledge was that he would be president for all of the people, and not the president of a privileged segment of this culturally diverse nation. Many Americans and people of the world are having serious adjustment problems with the change in leadership and philosophy. The idea of hope has taken its place in this land of moral decline. Outside of the realm of mortal thinking and practice, I am a profound believer that President Obama is an idea whose time has come out of Divine Order. The world, as it was created, has veered from its path of the four foundational underpinnings: Righteousness, Mercy, Justice, and Love. In the absence of these four tenants, a moral revival becomes necessary.

My faith in the America that I extol is stated in the proclamation of the Psalmist: "weeping may remain for the night, but rejoicing comes in the morning." The signs are clear; we are coming through the night with expected joy in the morning. After years in the wilderness, we can look upon the prophetic words of President Obama, who stands on faith and hope for the joy in the morning. After weathering the Bush/Chaney years of secrecy and distrust behind the doors of closed government that defied the people, we can now breath the fresh air of positive change in a government for the people. There are signs of evidence in the freedom the American people now experience. This freedom is fully accompanied by God's promise to the faithful, and a President who has put the country first in the dispensation of his duties. Here-to-fore, it appears that many of our past presidents have supported those who are privileged with economic wealth, and those of greater influence in places of power. The Obamaian philosophy gives attention to the forgotten, and those who suffer at the outer fringes of power. However, this is unwanted change for the conservative and privileged sector of the country, because the Obama Administration is striving to give the American people a level and equitable playground.

There is much hope in this new day, because there is a major difference in the order of politics. The president began his term extending himself across the political aisle in an effort to work with the Republican Party in demonstrating "One America." This effort has not been successful because it appears that anything that President Obama does is criticized and rejected without an offered alternative from his detractors. There seems to be no real desire for Republicans to coalesce with Democrats, which negates the effort of bridging the divide. As long as the American leadership is divided

we weaken any possibility of exhibiting strength abroad to our enemies or to would be global allies. We suffered this experience during
the Bush/Cheney years of negatives and distrust. The hope for the
future of America is that we extend our friendship to friend and foe,
with the understanding that when we are threatened we will act deci-
sively in our defense. That hope has begun under President Obama's
presidency, and we have begun some early inroads of working
together on the globe. His assumption of office has ushered in new
and refreshing world hope, freedom for all of humanity, regardless
of nationality, race or culture.

I am deeply encouraged that President Obama negated pursuing
the office of President by accentuating the African American Race
or any other special group of his choice. His willingness to represent all Americans regardless of their persuasions, politics, religions
or ethnicity is admirable. Many contributing Americans have been
disregarded and overlooked because of their lack of privilege. Once
more, it is time that the United States Constitution be studied and
adhered to in the fellowship of humanity in America.

I am grateful and fortunate to have ventured in travel to every
continent on the globe except Antarctica. These travels are under the
auspices of the United States Department of State where I serve as
a special speaker on the subjects of Democracy, Human Rights, and
Nonviolence as an Agent to Social Change. In my varied travels I
have seen and interacted with multiple cultures where I have been
received passionately as a friend of good will, and to my shame I
was reminded of the arrogance and uncaring attitude of the Bush
Administration..

America has a second chance to claim her world leadership
under the practiced aegis of righteousness, justice, mercy and
love. This is only possible when we are rescued from the turbulent waters of greed, hate and self-arrogance, and find comfort on
the dry fertile land of justice with respect for our fellow human
beings. Some perceived Michelle Obama's provocative comment as
a political and racist statement when she said **"For the first time
in my adult life I am proud of my country because it feels like
hope is finally making a comeback."** She was unjustly criticized
for her comment and was talked into apologizing, but those who

criticized her comment have not the slightest idea of what her life's journey had been up to the point of her comment. She sounded the clarion for many African American people, especially when you think back on the cold blooded Mississippi murder of the fourteen year old Emmitt Louis Till by two White men because he allegedly whistled at a white woman, and countless other murders of the same sort. There are accounts of African Americans and white men having been killed for attempting to assist African Americans in registering to vote in the American process, the heinous murder of Medgar Evers who was killed for assisting African Americans in voter registration, the torching of my grandmother's family home by the Ku Klux Klan and my parents being treated in a non-humane manner by local White store clerks. I can remember clothes shopping in department stores, and being denied the opportunity to try on garments for size because of my race and also being denied a cool drink of water from a fountain that was labeled "White only." It makes Michelle Obama's comment relevant and acceptable when African Americans had to inform their children that they could not accommodate their requests to visit white public amusement parks because of the color barrier. These mentions are just the tip of the iceberg of injustice throughout the lives of many African Americans. It is totally unfortunate that European Americans have never been interested in knowing African Americans as they experience life in a White ordered world. I remain convinced that, in our humanness, were we taught to experience one another's lives, we would discover the tolerance for coexistence. So, Michelle Obama sees hope on the way with the election of her fair and equitable minded husband, and many White and African American people of good will who are ready for change.

The United States of America has always lived up to national challenges, i.e., World War II, The Great Depression of 1929, medical hurdles such as the defeat of polio, smallpox, and tuberculosis, government programs for socially disadvantaged persons, and major employment programs for the unemployed. During the Great Depression, between 1935 and 1943, President Franklin Delano Roosevelt created the Work Projects Administration – WPA – that was an ambitious attack on American unemployment. The

WPA provided approximately eight million jobs in the construction of public buildings, projects and roads, fed children and redistributed food, clothing and housing. Anyone who needed help was eligible. America overcame this point and time of need, which was an example of a nation with the will to survive under perilous times. At the writing of this book, the American people are experiencing another time of trials and strain in our total social order; however, we will overcome once more because of our resilience. We are fortunate to have a President who lives with great hope. In a recent address to the United States Congress he lifted a nation with his optimism of better days ahead, but with a forceful call to the American people for action and an appeal for tough choices. He further called America to pull together and take responsibility for our future once more. With this boldness taken to heart, we can do the impossible.

We have come to the cutting edge of hope in America. During the period of World War II, the country was as close to being united as ever before or after. While the men and some woman served on the battlefields of Europe and the Pacific, American women assumed the helm at home and performed the jobs that had been traditionally held by men. There was an aura of patriotism and a spirit of winning the war. America believed that this was just, and there appeared to be no public expressions of dissatisfaction with our involvement. Even in the fields of entertainment we sang "When the Lights Go On Again All Over the World" because World War II was a long war that drained us of our youth and many resources that found their place as part of the military war implements. We are, once more, at a point of exhaustion with the wars in Iraq and Afghanistan. It is our hope that the lights will go on again, and the world will enjoy peace and tranquility everywhere.

It is the ghastly word "fear" that takes its place in the hearts and minds of insecure people in any given situation or region of the world. Iran is afraid of not having nuclear power so it is fortified to warrant off any possible military attack, or advance war, North Korea has brought itself to that same position, and it is alleged that Pakistan is also fortifying itself in a nuclear way. So, when does it end and how many lives will be lost before we come to our senses? While our concern must be for the United States of America, we must be concerned about the world at large, because of our inter-relatedness to the balance of humanity. Much of our behavior is observed by others, and to some degree, emulated. What we do, and how we do it, can make a positive or negative difference beyond our shores. When I travel the globe, I talk about the freedom and democracy that we practice in America. In addition, I speak so that for foreign countries to learn of our constitution and how we live within it. Many of my travels take me to places where freedom of speech, free press, and freedom of religion are totally unlawful. Even with our faults we live in a land where we have the freedom to grow and develop to our fullest potential.

Alexis de Tocqueville, a nineteenth century French scientist, historian and politician, expanded his vision of the America that means so very much to Americans when we wrote:[1]

"America is a land of wonders in which everything is in constant motion and every change seems an improvement...No natural boundary seems to be set to the efforts of man; and in his eyes, what is not yet done is only what he has not yet attempted to do."

It was Tocqueville's passionate vision that endeared this great country to its patriots, and those who held this land to be great in all of its endeavors. This is the reason we must, together, support the democratic way of life by helping in all ways to bridge the divide that keeps us from being what our forefathers intended in crafting the constitution. It is our duty to concern ourselves with supporting a balanced education for every American child, regardless of race or culture so that we improve literacy on every level. We should take advantage of our political process by becoming part of the influence to assure better and more accountable government, and utilize forums, conferences, religious congregations, work groups and places of human assemblies to advance friendly dialogue on the strength in unity. America, in its recent election of an African American President, is ripe for examining our differences and approaches to interrelatedness.

I am involved in facilitating dialogue on race and culture for racially mixed groups all over the world, and in our discussions I have witnessed that people, regardless of race and culture, have more in common than not. When we engage in honest discussion about backgrounds, personalities, behaviors, basic learning development and home training, it appears that we are not that much unalike. Some of the probing questions that I have used in discussions are as follows:

- Describe your background – race, gender, ethnicity, age, etc.

- Were you brought up in a formal religion?

- How much of a role did religion play in your life?

- Did both parents raise you?

- What was/were your parent's occupation/s?

- How would you describe your family income level for most of your youth?

- During your development years, were you ever exposed to different races and cultures?

- Where did your grandparents come from?

- Can you name the languages spoken in your home during your growing up years?

- What was the highest level of school you completed?

These are general questions that can be asked of anyone, no matter who they are, and, in comparison, the responses will produce a common base for positive relationships. This is where the work of bridging the divide begins. When we discover that we have more in common than not, we have the basis for coming together. With this approach, there is hope beyond the barriers that divide us.

When I was growing up in the Deep South, New Orleans, Louisiana, we lived in an African American ghetto, where White merchants primarily supplied goods and services. Many of these merchants lived in our community in housing units that were on the floors above their shops and we played with their children until the age of twelve years; the White parents, because of the color difference, abruptly ended our relationships up to that point. The ending of relationships was hurtful for the White children as well as for us because of our innocence. It was not long before we came to understand that the racial barrier was raised at the age of twelve or before.

In many cases the divide in southern living between the races was regrettable to all involved, but the man made laws of segregation governed our behavior. Many springs and summers have come and gone since much of the hard segregated behavior has been evidenced, and it is good to recognize that many people of good will have grown weary of the old ways. We have worked, African American and White people together, toward a better America with much progress. It is sad that there are still some vestiges of the old practices. I remain steadfastly hopeful that we are in a new day when good and sound reasoning will overtake the narrow mindedness of the practices, overt and covert, that keeps us from being the great American people we are.

In the invincible words of the late Reverend Martin Luther King, Jr., "The racial problem will be solved in American to the degree that every American considers himself personally confronted with it. Whether one lives in the heart of the Deep South or on the periphery of the North, the problem of injustice is his problem; it is his problem because it is America's problem."

CHAPTER IX

RECLAIMING OUR AMERICAN VALUES

****

*If a nation values anything more than freedom, it will lose its
freedom; and the irony of it is that if it is comfort or money
that it values more, it will lose that too.*

William Somerset Maugham

In a bold statement made by our President Barack Obama, at the
end of his first State of the Union address, "In the end it is our
ideals, our values, that built America—values that forge a nation
made up of immigrants from every corner of the globe, values that
drive our citizens still…unfortunately, too many of our citizens have
lost faith that our biggest institutions—our corporations, our media
and yes, our government—still reflect these same values…" This
observation of lost values is at the very core of America's dysfunctional state. Many of us have often mused about the good old days,
and how better the times were in relationships, and organizational
behavior. We remember how business was conducted, and hon-
ored with a handshake in the absence of a signed contract. We also
remember how neighbors supported one another in difficult times,
which is anchored in the scriptures, Matthew 7:12 "Do unto others
as you would have them do unto you." To value another as you value

yourself brings about respect and harmony, and the understanding of how to live and let live in the broader social order.

No period of our existence has ever been without disagreement or dispute, but there have been times that adherence to our value system supercedes any major disruptive behavior. I distinctly remember the rallying behind the American military during World War Two, and how we participated in the purchase of war bonds, and the replacement of men with women in the construction trades, Rosie the Riveter is a cultural icon of the United States. American humor depicted women who did the traditional work of men before who had been called to serve in the armed services. The women worked in factories, munitions plants, and war implements. This kind of support was indicative of America's commitment to maintaining our freedom and liberty.

These were the days of clean airwaves that produced radio's golden age shows, such as, Corliss Archer, Henry Aldrich, Our Miss Brooks, The Great Gildersleeve, Fibber McGee and Molly, and Amos and Andy. These were hard years for Americans. Part of this time was during the active depression of 1929 – 1941, when people eliminated luxuries, and concentrated on their needs. The radio took them beyond their troubled times with great hope. There was no time to focus on anything but survival. However, many people came closer together and shared their resources in demonstrations of support for one another. In later years I am reminded of the catastrophic snow on Chicago, Illinois in 1967. The city was torn asunder by civil rights demonstrations during the summer of 1966, however, when human need became evident, people of diverse backgrounds came together, not allowing their divisions and differences to stand between them, and helped to assuage the suffering. The same is reported about the perils that devastated the Gulf States in the aftermath of hurricane Katrina. Humanity served its best in helping those who were harmed. This is the human connectedness that was intended in the story of creation. From the caring teachings of Jesus, as he taught his disciples on the Mount of Olives: *"For I was hungry, and you gave me food, I was thirsty, and you gave me water, I was a stranger, and you took me in; I was naked, and you gave me clothes, I was sick, and you visited me, I was in prison, and you came to see me...Inasmuch as you have done it unto one of the least of these my brethren, you have done it unto me."* The demonstration of this spirit gives strength to the human soul, and builds the bridge to one another creating the family of brotherhood and sisterhood. John Donne, the sixteenth century English Jacobean poet, preacher, and major representative of the metaphysical poets of the period, once penned in his impoverished days, "No Man Is An Island." He said "Human beings do not thrive when isolated from others." With the advance of this thought, we should strive to go beyond "self" and search in the existence of others for our commonality that makes us one by nature, with humble respect for our individuality.

We must come together in the realization that in our unity we are more powerful than the individual. The integration of our different mind contributions to an idea gives us the ability to enhance our lives and the environment in which we reside. No one individual has ever been able to realize a great accomplishment without the help and assistance of another. With their craftiness and imagination, the architects of our U.S. Constitution did not write and sign the documents with a divided country in mind. They wrote a binding manifesto that was intended to bring all Americans under fair and cooperative orders. Further, the intent was to form a respectful government of the people, by the people, and for the people.

We are, here and now, at a point and time to do a strong bit of introspection of our inner beings in an act of ascertaining our strengths and weaknesses, and to resolve the truths on which this country was founded. In this time of division in these United States, our resolve has to be to move toward a more healed nation, and once again accept with dignity the title, "The Leader of the Free World."

While many undeveloped countries in Africa, Asia, South America, the Pacific Islands, and other countries looked to America for a bright ray of hope, that notion is changing. The world is revealing a dreary outlook, and wondering whether we can be believable anymore, since we have transmitted a divided country while losing our respectability around the world. I believe we can turn this perception around, and become, once more, the friendly nation we really are.

We can overcome the stigma of arrogance, disrespectfulness, and unscrupulous greed, with the help of our public religious institutions when they assume their rightful responsibility of shaping the minds of the millions of faith seekers who seek wholeness in their lives. I refer to churches, synagogues, mosques, and all places of religious assembly; places where we hope to find truth and moral principles taught instead of entertainment theaters of great oratory and music.

Reclaiming the values of America is a mammoth nationwide effort, which begins in each individual family guided by a common agenda that extends into schools of learning, factories, executive offices, and the faith community.

Writing of reclaiming America is not to be construed with those qualities that brought us shame and disgrace, but with the values that were cherished and practiced and that we adorned with pride. God Bless America, America the Beautiful, and the National Anthem were sung with ownership and meaningful expression. This is not to ignore the fact that we were fraught with problems, because history has recorded our struggles as a people from far away lands ensconced in our respective cultures, who transported our prejudices with us, Some born out of fear, and some out of ignorance. The fact still remains, when the nation is threatened, we rise to the occasion of collective support. In the aftermath of the destruction by Hurricane Katrina, America was there in the Gulf Coast and parts of the interior of New Orleans, Louisiana. The American people, also, rose to the occasion when the terrorist struck the World Trade Center in New York City, and they have gone to far distant lands to protect and defend our interest in world humanity, and human rights.

Reclaiming the values that matter to us becomes an important factor in reversing the scheme of much of the shame, and selfish greed that has cropped up in our land over the past century. We should look with disdain on the sordid behavior of many of our legislative representatives, members of the religious clergy, those who have occupied some of the most sought after, and prestigious offices of the land. We have been a blessed nation in spite of our misdeeds, and we have lived and taken the good life for granted. The future of the country depends on how we are perceived by the world, and whether we have been good stewards in our responsibility as trusted keepers of the land. In the magnificent creation story, it was God's intent that man would have complete charge of the earth (Genesis 2:26) We have no way to go but return to the natural order that was meant for our lives. To reclaim the good values and virtues of our land is close to Godliness, and His first thought of our purpose.

Material cravings capture the soul of man, and reorder his mission. He sometimes becomes blinded to those things that are good, and preoccupied by the trappings of evil. Reclaiming our basic values in America can be the rightful pathway back to God. We can begin with common respect and decency for all human beings, positive regard for family life, the assurance of a clean environment, making the education of our children a communitywide initiative, so we might plan for and guard the future, sanitize the air waves, and media print for the developmental health of all humanity, and make a practice of moral behavior.

Reclaiming the values of America assumes that we made a good and worthwhile start in the development of this land in whatever was sane, positively enhancing, aware of one another's presence, and attending to needs. We should consider reviewing and applying those principles for going forward. Keep in mind, America was realized by people who were seeking their independence from a tyrannical government in a new land where they could breath freely. The time to do an introspective view of ourselves is now, opening ourselves to change for a life that is unencumbered with superficial oddities of perceived power and popularity.

Sometimes decisions to be made that are good for us are difficult to come by at best, however, again in the prophetic words of Martin Luther King, Jr., when decisions have to be made:

"**Cowardice** asks the question is it safe, **Vanity** asks the question is it popular,
Expediency asks the question is it politic, But conscience asks the question is it right?
There comes a time when one takes a position that is neither safe, nor popular, nor
Politic, but because conscience tells him that it is right."

CHAPTER X

IN SEARCH OF UNITY

****

Pour the sweet milk of concord into hell, Uproar the universal peace, confound All unity on earth.

William Shakespeare

In the Divine Order of the universe, humanity was created to be in harmonious relationships with one another so we might have strength and capacity to further enhance
God's kingdom on earth. Somehow we have lived outside of this Divine plan to pursue our chosen paths. The paths we have chosen have been fraught with pain, sickness, stress, disappointment, and sometimes misdirected joy. We have become aliens to the principles we were intended. to follow. In the second chapter, and eighteenth verse of Genesis, God spoke, "It is not good that man should be alone. " and so he placed man in the company of another being which eventually multiplied into a community of humanity. To be in communion with like minds and spirits is God's way of assuring peace and solidarity.

In conceptualizing unity in the ranks of humanity, the hymnist, John Oxenham wrote these poignant words:

"In Christ there is no east or west, in Him no south or north; but one great fellowship of love throughout the whole wide earth.

Join hands then my brothers of faith, whatever your race may be; Who serves my father as a son is surely kin to me."[1]

David, the shepherd boy who was born to be a king, appears to have written these embracing words found in Psalms 133.

"How good and pleasant it is when brothers live together in unity! It is like precious oil poured on the head, running down on the beard, running down on Aaron's beard, down upon the collar of his robes. It is as if the dew of Hermon ere falling on Mount Zion. For there the Lord bestows his blessing, even life forevermore."

These rich and potent words should invoke a strong desire to do an introspection of our being, and where there is none, create and accept the path to the unification of the whole of humanity and discover the true meaning of peace. Historians have documented human divisions all over the globe. Tribal divisions have escalated to deathly conflicts and wars on the continent of Africa, cultural divisions between Albanians and Serbs continue to dominate lives in Kosovo, where war has claimed many lives, young and old, North and South Korea have yet to reach a peaceful accord, even with blood relatives on both sides, the smoldering differences between Irish Catholics and Protestants in Ireland, the Arabic and Jewish divide in the Middle East, and many more. On occasions of national disaster the introduction of a grand coalition government has been introduced in the face of governmental division. A coalition government exists when the two largest political parties come together in forming a coalition around common issues. There are times when threatening national circumstances require unified government attention. For the survival of our nation, the United States Government saw a need to bond during the Great Depression, World Wars I and II, and September 11, 2001. It is unfortunate that during times of normal peace our government finds difficulty working together in bridging whatever divides them. When government works in a cohesive manner, it sets the tone and behavior parameters for the people it governs. A few examples of global grand coalitions that have worked effectively are as follows:

Bulgaria - Socialist Party, the National Movement for Simeon II and the Movement for Rights and Freedoms – 2005-2009

Poland – Polish United Worker's Party, Democratic Party, and Peasants Party 1989 – 1990

U.S. Virgin Islands- Democratic Party, the Independent Citizens Movement and Independents – 2007

Kenya- Party of National Unity, and Orange Democratic Movement – 2007

These coalitions were formed out of disagreements and strife, but their formations have brought about much improved governmental order. Where there are differences in approaches and opinions to problem solving, there is no better approach than working in unity, and where common sense prevails.

For survival and success in this complex world, and where nations, large and small, race to build the most destructive weapons to protect themselves from outer harm, we have come to a point where we have abandoned God. We are attempting to make the journey all by ourselves. It is important to recognize our helplessness without the sovereignty of our creator.

I suggest the following three ways to achieve unity in a divided community:

Living on One Accord – Identify a common cause that all can agree to. According to the Acts of the Apostles, God's Spirit was manifested in a miraculous way on the day of Pentecost., (Acts 2), where diverse groups came together as one people, each speaking in his own language, but yet understanding the message of unity. Humanity is not so very different that common ground is not recognizable, and understood. Their spirits were completely under control of God's Holy Spirit; their words were the words of God. They found peace and brotherhood in a period of unity. This account of people coming together under one cause is not farfetched, but possible under willing conditions. While some biblical commentator, as in our day, thought these people had indulged in an over abundance of intoxicating wine. However, it was explained by the Apostle Peter that the 9:00 AM hour was much to early for wine babbling, as the fast was over at 10:00 AM..

There are many religious, social, and political issues that we can identify with, and find common agreement. This same God who brought unity to Pentecost is also able to bring unity among White, Black, Hispanic, Asian, Moslem, and the whole of earthly humankind. The difference in the happening on the day of Pentecost and the modern day world is that the people of different cultures and races of the Mediterranean world were open to positive change, and to the Holy Spirit working in their lives to enhance their lives by surviving together. We have the same obligation in moving out of our comfort zonesto create such unity.Reasoning Together – The wisdom of the prophet Isaiah called a divided people together According to Isaiah, the scripture reads,

Come now, let us reason together, says the Lord. Though your sins are like scarlet, they shall be as white as snow; though they are red as crimson, they shall be like wool.

If you are willing and obedient, you will eat the best from the land; but if you resist and rebel, you will be devoured by the sword." Notice the "will" to reason together is as important as any factor in seeking unity. It did not matter that their differences kept them apart, the point that is being made is God is a forgiving God, and He promised that were they obedient He would cleanse them of their sins, and they would be washed as white as snow, and unblemished with the stains of disobedience. Our land needs healing, no matter how much legislation is passed in our halls of law, it really doesn't matter who is president. Until we come together as a unified nation, this land will remain sick, and will not be healed.

During the aftermath of the 9/11 tragedy we witnessed unified American grief as never before, because we experienced our vulnerability, we suffered the same shock and fear. It is amazing how we can rally around tragedies by being there for one another, but we have trouble normalizing unity in everyday life. We are a nation with the motto, "In God We Trust," but are hard pressed to put it into practice. If Americans truly put our trust in God, and believe in His sovereignty, why aren't we a markedly a better nation? Why such drastic divisions on all fronts? Why can't we come together as the family of God?

Respecting Humanity – We are encouraged by our Creator to live in a bond of unity, because He does not love one of us or some of us more than others. God is balanced in his out pouring of love. In the book of Acts 10:34, Simon Peter spoke these words from the home of Cornelius, the Greek Centurion:

"Of a truth I perceive that God is no respecter of persons: But in every nation he that feareth Him, and worketh Righteousness is accepted with Him." It was made clear, through Peter, that the Good News of Christ is for everyone, and should not allow any barrier, language, culture, prejudice, geography, economic class or education keep us apart. The bell is tolling for us to answer the call to unity and solidarity even in our differences. Let us build together a community of love, trust, and faith, one that our children will be proud to emulate. If a child lives in a community without respect for persons, he will be disrespectful, if a child lives in a community of division and hate, he will live a life of confusion and violence, and if a child lives in a fragmented environment, he will not experience the wholeness that God intended.

Approximately 56 years ago I served as a principal participant in the great American civil rights movement of the 1950s and 60s. I was privileged to witness a preview of what is possible when diverse people of color, race, and culture come together and agree on a positive cause. The beginning was staged in Montgomery, Alabama. It is the place where Jefferson Davis in 1861, accepted the office of provisional president for the seceding confederate states that upheld slavery. This was a time of our American History that was a blatant mark against unity. In unity, there is something that is very liberating. My memory takes me back to the comforting words of an elderly black woman somewhere on a dusty roads of Alabama, as she demonstrated by walking in the memorable stride toward freedom. She was asked by a news reporter: "Mam, tell me how you feel walking in this demonstration, are you tired?" She said, "Son my feets is tired, but my soul is rested, cause we is walking to freedom together." Freedom is the benefit that God has provided for us to live in peace, harmony, and love, regardless of the views that we have about others who don't look, speak, or act as we do, It doesn't matter how we have made false judgments about one another there comes a time when we should come to recognize the intrinsic good in all of us, and rise to the occasion of extending agape love to the abused, the used, the forgotten, and the down-trodden. In the search for unity we will find its deepest roots in our spiritual nature. When individuals and communities are connected to the spiritual roots of the struggle, we are transformed from the jangling discords of our community to a beautiful symphony of brotherhood and sisterhood that is pleasing to almighty God. The Psalmist says, (133) "Behold, how good and how pleasant it is for brethren to dwell together in unity..."

CHAPTER XI

I DON'T FEEL NO WAYS TIRED

****

*The woods are lovely, dark, and deep, but I have promises to keep,
and miles to go before I sleep, and miles to go before I sleep.*

Robert Frost

The great nineteenth century imaginative poet seemed to have the ability to experience humanity during his day and the days ahead, in putting forth the effort to shape our destiny. There are those of us who recognize our life's purpose early enough to discipline the journey ahead to bring about the result we seek. According to the gospel of John Jesus teaches, "I must work the works of him that sent me, while it is day: the night cometh, when no man can work." The lesson encourages us to recognize our purpose, and work toward the goal while there is still time. Success has no claim for the weary wonderer, but is given to those who stay the course, even through weathered times.

The year 1619 is indelible in the minds of historians, and African Americans, down through the generations, who remember that the first Africans docked at Jamestown, Virginia on a Dutch Ship called "Man-of-War." They began their lives in the new land under the aegis of indentured servitude owning land. However, greed among the White plantation owners outgrew humility inhuman slavery was crudely introduced for the next 200 years. It has been said that the souls of African American people were created to endure times of hardship. Life for African Americans is fraught with the rigors of life, and with an undeniable exclusion from positions of preference. The books of the Old Testament teach us that the Israelites were always being chided by God, and taught by the prophets, because of their disobedience to God's commands, however, He referred to them as the chosen people, He forgave, and blessed them. As African Americans study scriptures in the Old Testament, there is an immediate Jewish identity, which comes to mind. Will the Messiah come from Black people of Africa? This is a wait - and - see response.

I have a great memory of my maternal grandmother and me, sitting on her porch in Mississippi shelling peas. I loved these times I spent with her, because these were the times she would share life's experiences with me. She told me a little story about the times African American people went through during the great depression of 1929, She said, "as many people of wealth and means experienced times of devastation, because they lost what they had, many African Americans found themselves on a different plain by the experience of not losing what you don't have." It was a time to make do with the little that was entrusted to you. There were vegetable gardens, and livestock for food, the ability to build shelter from scrap wood, clothing made from feed sacks, and education from dedicated teachers, who were not paid much, but cared enough to instill pride, and a hunger for learning. It was about survival, and faith and hope for a brighter tomorrow. Langston Hughes captivated "endurance" in a meaningful poem that gives strength to encouragement.

Mother To Son

Well son, I'll tell you: Life for me ain't been no crystal stair.
It's had tacks in it, and splinters, and boards torn up,
And places with no carpet on the floor—Bare. But all the time
I'se been a-climbin' on, And reachin' landin's, and turning corners,
And sometimes goin' in the dark Where there ain't been no light
So boy, don't you turn back. Don't you set down on the steps.
Cause you finds it's kinder hard. Don't you fall now—
For I'se still goin' honey, I'se still climbin,'
And life for me ain't been no crystal stair.

Hughes wrote a powerful word for anyone who struggles with the adversities of life's many obstacles, and is destined to overcome. It is encouraging to those who have thoughts of giving up but who understand that the cost for giving up is much too great. Any worthwhile struggle comes with sacrifice, and a great desire to accomplish the goal that is sought. Life, for many African American people has been over laden with strife and uncertain times; however endurance has been a major part of sustaining in spite of hardships. Faith in God and endurance have served as a guarantee in overcoming tough times. Religion, though learned from White people, has been the bridge that connected suffering to freedom. "The Promised Land," has a meaning of going to a place that is free of prejudice, hate, inequality, fear and racism. That is why endurance is so very important, while becoming tired is not an option. There is no rest for the weary, but there is fullness of life for the strong hearted.

The mere fact that African Americans continue to be a viable part of the American story, says much for the lasting scientific, technological, social, political, and many other contributions made over the last 400 years. It is with this kind of fortitude, in spite of obstacles, that these scorned Americans will usher in the much-needed salvation that will free the United States of America from the grip of the world community, and herself. It will be then, and only then we can sing "God Bless America" with new meaning. No proclamation of social and racial improvement would be accurate without acknowledging the fraction of good that has been done, since the landing at Jamestown, Virginia. However, as penned by Robert Frost, "we have many miles to go before we sleep." America can and will be blessed with freedom for all of her people when we she comes to respect the preservation of God given life, and see each human being as an integral part of the human family. Freedom comes to open hearts and minds that are ready for new and whole experiences with the unknown and unfamiliar. Fear and ignorance impede genuine relationships that have the potential for developing true communities of love understanding. From the pen of Alfred Tennyson, "Tis better to have loved and lost than never to have loved at all." We all cheat ourselves of life's many adventures when we miss the advantage of expanding relationships.

Humanity will never fully benefit from the purpose for which it was created until relationships are realized unconditionally. In its diversity, America has the potential for being the world's paradigm for racial and cultural harmony. Unfortunately, our nation has not enjoyed sustained leadership that is committed to diminishing the walls of racial, cultural, and gender inequity. The discussion of the celebrated ringing of the freedom bell in America will continue until we come to realize the true purpose for our creation. . President Barack Hussein Obama is an emphatic example of the hopes and aspirations that have been held in the hearts of the African American people when they realized they were a part of this new world. This would not have happened if they surrendered to fatigue and gave up. The President has given hope the true meaning of possibilities.

It is laudable, it's exciting, it's wonderful that America has come to being able to look beyond color to bring about needed change in the social order. However, this much talked about change can only take hold when positive influence is wielded by dedicated leaders who believe in the strength of a unified community. We have come much too far to tire of the journey. We yearn for peace and improved understanding of what we do not know, but are willing to know. We are fortunate that there are more people of good will in our midst who need to stand and be counted for their rightful opinions.

While we now have a president who demonstrates equitable leadership, he needs the support of every American to advance the cause of freedom and equality throughout the land. Business, labor, halls of education, communities of faith, public places of assembly, political elected officials, law enforcement types, and children of all ages should be taught and practice equitable ways of living in a diverse America. This is the beginning of peace, and true human development. Our energies are being used to separate instead of uniting. Let us conserve our energy for the important and lasting work of creating the "Beloved Community."

Frederick Douglass, in a speech on John Brown, wrote, "No man fails, or can fail, who so grandly gives himself and all he has to a righteous cause." Freedom is the desire and goal of any human being who has God endowed entitlements to the riches of life. The legislative trail of the struggle for civil rights can be traced as far back as1776 under the penmanship of Thomas Jefferson when he wrote most of the Declaration of Independence. Some will argue as to whether this document limited itself to the thirteen colonies or was it meant to be all inclusive of all men.

The realization that comes to mind is, if African American men were regarded as chattel, then the language used in the Declaration of Independence is exclusive of African Americans. In 1865, the thirteenth Amendment to the Constitution abolished slavery but did not provide equal opportunity to African Americans. The Civil Rights Act of 1866 is still contested by the demagogues of racial and cultural separation. This act was ratified on April 9, 1866 after President Andrew Johnson vetoed it. The declaration of the act delineated that all persons born in the United States, regardless of race, color, or condition were citizens. Citizenship provided the right for each to make and enforce contracts, to sue…to inherit, purchase, lease, sell, hold, and convey real and personal property, and to full and equal benefit of all laws and proceedings for the security of persons and property, as enjoyed by White citizens…While legislation is an important aspect of governance and order, it is an impossibility to legislate morality. It is believed that most Americans are law-abiding citizens who uphold justice by doing what is right, and avoiding evil.

There are lessons to be learned from historical experiences in the lives of our forbearers who have been up against life' obstacles.Our lives are enriched, shaoed and influenced by the sacrifices of Jesus.. Martin Luther King, Jr., in his desire to influence positive social change joined the ranks of martyrs who seemed to be inexhaustible in their quest for the goal they sought. Geoffrey Chaucer, the fourteenth century writer, is given to the saying, "Nothing ventured, nothing gained." This saying is akin to a fourteenth century proverb: Qui onques rien n'enprist riens n'achieva (He who never undertook anything never achieved anything). There is no gain for growing tired in the pursuance of a worthwhile goal.

Joe Darion wrote the lyrics to "The Impossible Dream," from "Man of La Mancha." In his capture of pursuing what appears to be impossible without faith, he wrote:

"To dream the impossible dream
To fight the unbeatable foe
To bear with unbearable sorrow
To run where the brave dare not go...

And the world will be better for this
That one man, scorned and covered with scars
Still strove with his last ounce of the human divide begins with a
Divine faith that transcends all doubts, fears, prejudices, courage
To reach the unreachable star."[1]

This inexhaustible faith has the possibility of diminishing our current inability to recognize our commonalities, and also a chance to come to know and appreciate one another as we truly are.

Here is a true story of a man, whom I met in New Orleans, Louisiana, when I was a thirteen-year-old elementary school student, by the name of Matthew Alexander Henson, an African American. In 1950 my teacher took our class to the dedication of the gymnasium at Dillard University where the gymnasium was dedicated in the name of Henson. We were told, at the time, Henson accompanied Admiral Robert Perry on his Arctic exploration in discovering the North Pole. Many years later, I learned that the discovery was controversial when endless discussions took place as to whether Peary made the discovery or Henson. The job that was reserved for Henson, due to segregation of the races, was valet to Peary until it was learned that Henson possessed dog sled handling skills, plus his fluency in the Inuit Indian language was a bonus to the expedition. After debilitating rigors with the sub zero weather, and warming of ice floats, success was doubtful at times, however they continued the exhausting expedition.

While Peary was driven in his quest to be the first man to discover the North Pole, he sent Bob Bartlett, the commander of the ship, back to Cape Columbia, and he would continue the trip with Henson. It was later learned that Peary did not want to share the discovery with anyone else. Henson and the Inuit Indians did not count, because of the race issue. Peary suffered from leukemia, and was forced to ride in one of the dog sleds while Henson forged ahead and made the discovery alone to, Peary's chagrin. This abbreviated story is an example how success comes to those who are dedicated to a cause without tiring. Today Matthew Alexander Henson is remembered as a great man who endured to the bitter end in spite of deception and rejection.

There is something mystical about the civil rights song, "We shall overcome," because when you set your mind toward a goal, and claim it before it is obtained, it will be achieved before it is realized. It is a fact, the story of the African American people will serve as the American epilogue in overcoming the dangers, toils, and snares of hard times, we have already come.

The poor, the disallowed and disavowed, the forgotten and the maligned constantly ask the question, "How long?" The answer was given in the text of what appeared to be a Divine Ordered speech by the late Martin Luther King, Jr. at the end of the great march from Selma to Montgomery, Alabama: "How long? Not long, because the arc of the moral universe is long, but it bends toward justice." While it has been almost four hundred years in our wait for justice, we can never tire of the quest. It is a mandatory response, "I Don't Feel No Ways Tired."

The Montgomery Bus Boycott of 1955 and 56 was a deliberate attempt to demonstrate perseverance of a people who had become worn down with the heat and pressure of oppression, but not too tired to stand up for justice. Their spiritual adrenaline, at peak point, gave them the impetus to sacrifice their comfort for a future of respect and dignity. The desire to exercise all of the freedoms that life guarantees.

Human beings were created to withstand the rigors of the world, and to rebound with faith during times of discouragement. The Christian ethic fortifies and models the strength of a determined people. This is a lesson for all people who find themselves beset under oppressive measures. Many military prisoners of war have weathered some of the most harrowing circumstances, and survived because of the faith and will to remain strong in spite of the undue pressure. Presidential hopeful John McCain has lived with his gruesome memories of five and one half years in a North Vietnamese prison. The treatment he received was, in his words unbearable, and he was almost at the point of suicide. He developed the inner fortitude to overcome his captor's treatment, and walked out of prison to live out his life. Determination for a cause will supply every need to overcome adversity. The Negro Spiritual truly attests to "I Don't Feel No Ways Tired."

CHAPTER XII

YOU TOO CAN
MAKE A DIFFERENCE

****

If a man does not keep pace with his companions, perhaps it is
because he hears a different drummer. Let him step to the music
he hears, however measured or far away.

Henry David Thoreau

Quite often I have been asked what one can do to assist in bringing about needed change in our social order. There are many persons who have willing hearts to do something significant, but are at a loss as to what they can do. We are fortunately blessed to be gifted with different talents, some more than others, however, we have talents that can be put to use for the betterment of our lives. I am reminded of a story I once heard. It is found in biblical scriptures, (John 6:5-13). This story is centered around a young unassuming boy who resided in the rural countryside with his parents outside of the Mid Eastern city of Galilee. In those days Galilee was a tranquil fishing village, where the fields were ripe for the harvest with vegetation and plant life. Banana trees and citrus fruit groves covered the landscape. It was mostly green hills, and open space, Monuments, the Synagogue, and other sites of interest.

This story, with a few significant variations, follows the tradition of the feeding of the multitude in the other three gospels, Matthew,

Mark, and Luke. In the gospel of John there are several points of departure from which this magnificent story can be told: (1) The plight of that teaming multitude caught in the clutches of a damnable religio-socio predicament, (2) The great compassion of Jesus for a people who were up against hard times, or (3) The terrible un-readiness of the disciples for the great happening that was about to come. It seems most appropriate to identify the work of Jesus, with His miraculously transformed and expanded matter. In this scripture, He teaches His disciples a lesson in unconditional faith when there appears to be no way out of an impossible situation. The miracle of feeding five thousand plus persons was unlike any other miracle that Jesus did. All the other miracles can be seen as miracles of transformation. In His transforming miracles He changed water into fine wine, He healed the man with the withered hand, He cured the nobleman's son, and He raised Jairus' daughter from the dead. This act that Jesus caused in the feeding of the multitude of people by using five barley loaves, and two tiny fish was, indeed, a miracle of expansion. He took what was, and expanded what was into infinitely more of what was, and the end product in its is- ness maintained its was- ness.

He started out with a little borrowed lunch that was prepared somewhere in the rustic hills of Galilee. The core of the story features a little boy who had been permitted by his parents, for the first time, to venture outside of his rural setting to the city of Galilee. He had reached a reasonable age that gave his parents comfort to trust him to travel to Galilee alone. Before, he had been accustomed to being chaperoned by his parents. This time was markedly different.

When he received permission to go, he was terribly excited, and somewhat beside himself. After - all, he was growing up to be responsible, and reliable. The evening before his trip he made up his anticipated busy itinerary. He would visit the Synagogue, and the historical monuments, he would visit the market square and watch the merchants sell their goods, he would go to the fishermen's wharf, and watch them cast their nets for a catch, and about noon time he would find himself a big shade tree and have him self a little lunch. He tossed with excitement all nightlong, and early the next morning he rose a little before day- break. His mother carefully prepared him a little lunch of five barley loaves, and two tiny fish. She gave him last minute instructions, and a big hug, and sent him on his way. He started out walking, and then he would skip a while, and then he would run fast for a few yards. When he arrived at the edge of the city he began to hear murmuring sounds of the city people, he could smell the aroma of fresh fruits, baked goods, and fresh fish. As he got nearer, he saw a large mass of rushing humanity in a big hurry, going to a place of interest. At last, he was in the city. In his excitement he almost forgot his itinerary, as he became distracted by a large multitude of people amassed on a hillside near the Sea of Galilee. They seemed engrossed in a large meeting. The crowd intrigued the boy, so he found himself joining them out of curiosity. When he drew closer he noticed that the multitude was of mountainous proportion, and people were giving their undivided attention to some man who seemed to be a great pulling power, who was situated at the top of the crowd.

The boy could hear the uttering of the crowed. Some were saying of the man:

"He just healed a man at the pool of Bethesda." Others were saying:

"He calmed the wind storm on the Sea of Galilee."

"He talked to a Samaritan woman at Jacob's Well."

By this time the boy was surely confused. He wondered who the **"He"** was of whom the crowd was speaking. Why was **"He"** the topic of everyone's conversation? He began to worm his way around the five footers, and the six footers, the fat and the skinny ones until he was able to see the man who was surrounded by twelve other men. He seemed to be at debate with His enemies; the Scribes and the Pharisees. When the debate was exhausted Jesus, **the man**, lifted up His eyes, and saw a great company come unto Him, and He said to Philip, "Where shall we buy bread that these may eat?" Philip answered Him: "Two hundred pennyworth of bread is not sufficient for them…even if each took a little." Jesus said to His Disciples, "Go and see if there is any food among these people."

They went out through the multitude looking for food, rank upon rank, file upon file finding nothing. When they returned, Andrew told Him: "There is a boy here which has five barley loaves, and two tiny fish, but that is not enough for all of these people." Jesus said to Andrew, "bring the boy to me." Andrew went back to the boy, and said, "son, Jesus wants your lunch," and the boy said, "Sir, Jesus can have anything I've got." Then Jesus took the five barley loaves and the two tiny fish and gave thanks to almighty God. When He finished praying He gave the food to the disciples, and they fed the multitude. This miracle could not have happened until the boy gave the barley loaves and fish from his hands to the hands of Jesus. If you can get it out of your hands into His hands, He can do more with it than you can in your hands.

From the faith perspective, we can give Jesus our trials and tribulations, or anything that becomes problematical, and with a believable prayer life.ezperience, miraculous changes occur that brings a better meaning to your life. I write of this from true and proved experience, and that is why I can be assured that the divide that we are experiencing will be bridged as an answer to unconditional prayer. While it is desirable to have many to pray for a cause, God hears and acts on the prayers of any one individual, and as the story emphasized it did not take a multitude of people to provide the fundamental food for the five thousand, God used one little boy to work His miracle. You too can make a difference.

As Robert Browning once wrote: " A man's reach should exceed his grasp, or what's a heaven for." We share a complex world that is bursting with challenges. A world where demand is high, and supply is sometimes questionable. We are experiencing a time of advanced technology where at the touch of a computer button great results are brought forth that can affect a total environment, and change our way of living. The future belongs to oncoming generations who must always be at the ready to meet new challenges in the world that is ever evolving with new ideas, changing trends, and bigger and better products.

Given this ever - changing society, we can ill afford to continue on a divided path. We need all of the innovative, and advanced ideas that this nation can produce in an effort to sustain ourselves, and maintain our current achievements. Our youth of today are expected to do introspection of their abilities to take on a changing world where competition is becoming tougher. We can no longer put today off for tomorrow, because tomorrow is now. The careful sensitivity to the need for togetherness as a nation cannot be emphasized enough. We are all in this forward effort together. Every single individual must be counted in the total American equation. The wise investment of our time will bring great dividends in the future. We are making strides at closing the gaps that divide us, because it makes good sense. We are totally involved in changing times Our mandate for adjusting to change is before us, and we, together, must make a better world for us to thrive, share, and find a ground of harmony on which to live and share.

I celebrate, with great enthusiasm, the marked societal changes that have been made, I distinctly remember going to school, and not having the privilege of sharing my years of study with any other culture other than African American. I rode the public transport bus in the "Colored Section", drank from the public water fountains that were labeled "Colored Only, and the used school text books that were handed down by White students. These times have changed for the better, and we are all richer, in practice and spirit for it.

As we move on to greater heights and achievements in a unified manner, let us do it with full knowledge that, as a country, we will reap success in a bigger way. It has been said, and proved that success comes in **CANS not CAN'TS**. If we believe that we can achieve, yes we can. We often live in fear of the unknown and doubt our capability to conquer our fears and the unconquerable, but when we aim high enough and endure to the bitter end then we will realize that our aim was on target. Let us build the bridge together that unites us.

I have always had a high regard for time, and the parameter of time in which we are allotted to accomplish tasks that are important to our earthly survival. In the realm of time our moments are precious at best, and wise and prudent use of our time is an investment of riches that awaits bountiful dividends in the future. Time is not to be taken for granted, and squandered away, but to be guarded as space to be used in the praise and honor of God. In the scope of a lifetime, time is measured by what we accomplish within the limits we are given. Dr. Benjamin E. Mays understood the limits of his life, once said: " I have only just a minute. Only sixty seconds in it. I didn't seek it, and I didn't choose it but it is up to me to use it, suffer if I lose it, give account if I abuse it. I have just a tiny minute but eternity is in it." [1] In the span of life, time is very short, and we are given a definitive period to enhance our lives or that of others. However, we find it unfulfilling when we limit ourselves to a small segment of look-alikes in a community of God created human diversity. We have but to look beyond our immediate surroundings, and find those who are of different persuasions and looks, and we might discover we are not that much unalike. We were created to reflect on our precious gift of life, and how we can socialize with others on our journey. What would the world be if we were all the same? How would we expand our learning of our environment if everybody and everything were the same? I would dare say that we would shrink as violets and wither into oblivion of boredom and miss the chance to experience the true beauty of the earth, and the earth's inhabitants. I appeal to you to take seriously the societal make up of the coming years, and grow in unity - unity framed with the desire to do good, and avoid evil, while respecting the rights and privileges of our fellow beings We have the future of America in our hands. Let us move forward in this new age to bring about a new world order of respect for all human beings, and a cross fertilization of peace and goodwill.

CHAPTER XIII

BRIDGING THE DIVIDE

****

Do unto others, as you would have them do unto you.

Luke 6:31, NIV

The ethic of reciprocity gives rise to broader respect and dignity due to fellow beings. While we recognize that we do not occupy this earthly space alone, it is fitting to respect the presence of others and their will to exist in sharing the space we cover. Selfishness comes with our individual right to be ourselves; however we have not the right to deny another human being the same rights that we are entitled to. In the realization that we all find secured comfort in our own space, we must adhere to the fact that there are others who share the same feeling. However, we find ourselves in a broader community of coexistence and dependence with difficulty reconciling both realities.

For many of us, it is not easy to cohabit with those who do not share our philosophy or respect our values, and for many it is difficult to interact with those who do not share their same physical resemblance or language. America is not a nation of cohorts but is diverse in many races and cultures with a collectively written constitution that was written to protect our rights as the American people, regardless of ethnicity, race or country of origin. Since the alleged discovery of America over 500 years ago, it has been a struggle as to who has a right to exist here. Laws, creeds, resolutions, amendments and all manner of documents seeking to address the divisions of American inhabitants have been helpful in principle, but not so in practice. The practice of racial and cultural segregation is an American way of life, however, it is a way of life that is dispiriting in all respects, to the strength of the nation. On the globe, we appear vulnerable because we have no allegiance to a common principle as one people.

Bridging the Divide is a practiced study of making a broader attempt to cause the American people to do an introspective examination of their role in changing the anatomy of this nation from one that works against one another to one that works together. As human beings we should all be encouraged and proud of our individual ethnicity. We should take great pride in celebrating it with those we don't know. When the Irish and Italians came to these shores they were ostracized and chided in ways that made them feel unwelcome. Asians continue to be resisted, but because they are industrious they are tolerated. African Americans have never been welcomed except for their labor. There are many other cultures that have had tough times in America. The question continues to be raised, who are the American natives and where did they originate? According to the reports of Christopher Columbus, the alleged discoverer, so-called Indians were on the land upon his arrival, and if that were true, it would seem probable that the Indians are native to the land.

Much of history can be received as subjective depending upon who records it. Much of it is incomplete because of the limited knowledge of those who assume the credit for what has been found or discovered. Today we struggle with what we do not know, and what we don't know is the result of fear and ignorance. We have not truly begun to deeply understand the differences in human nature and the cultures and races within. The ignorance and fear continue to haunt our inability to seek further enhancement about the people we encounter on a daily basis, but do not know. The major problem that keeps us apart is that we make assumptions about the people we do not know and stereotypically label them. There are several approaches to learning more about people who cross our path, and if we know more about them and develop a more in-depth understanding about who they are, i t is possible that we will find more in common than not.

Nature has been configured by erosion shifts in earth's order, and in many cases, man has made attempts to bridge the chasms that separate land that could be more valuable for easier access. In the improvement of the delivery of commercial goods and services between far distant points, we have devised more convenient means of transport. The creative mind of man has forever found ways to shorten distances between expanding destinations of interest. Boats, airplanes, motored vehicles, bridges, all sort of connecting devices have enhanced our ability to connect when the need arises. The connecting of human nature has seemed to be the most difficult in all of our existence.

The barriers that keep us apart are stored in our inability to come to know one another.

We share the environment under the canopy of the blue skies, the sun, the wind, and the rain, but we do not share intimate knowledge of one another. We, as human beings, have more in common than not, however, we would rather live in the shadows of stereotypes, and false judgments than extend our beings in better relationships.

America is in need of an intercultural revival, a time of deep reflection on the needs of what it means and takes to create the beloved community. This is a time when the country needs dedicated and spiritual minds of committed moral leadership to be the bridge in bringing a new kind of relationship between races and cultures in positive relationships. This is no time for polite political patrician agendas, but a United States of America, indivisible with liberty and justice for all. My gratitude is extended to those who have attempted in many ways to bridge the divide, but were met with rejection or only short-term success. I believe the way to make the lasting difference is racial and cultural tolerance as a way of life that is taught, until it becomes a way of life throughout human development. I offer the following non-offensive approaches to entering the sphere of a better understanding of our peopled environment that will help bridge the cultural and racial divide:

We, as Americans, have come to recognize a new era of culturally diverse inhabitants who understand that their rights should not be abridged, and they are entitled to all that our country has to offer. We have always existed under a divided system, and it is difficult for some of our citizens to adapt to a changed way of living with others. Those of us who are outside of favorable opportunities, who have been disavowed, and disallowed, are creating public tensions that beckon the attention of those in the ruling class. This social divide necessitates a peaceful bridge that will usher in harmonious relationships, but not without the accoutrements that provide all a fair and equitable chance at making life work in the balance. This kind of coexistence is made possible when the transformation of right relationships is realized and respected between classes of people who recognize a new day. Those who have not been accustomed to a better life must make the necessary adjustments to find their way in the broader spectrum of society, and this can only happen by disciplined demand. In the words of Frederick Douglas, "...Power concedes nothing without demand, it never did, and it never will." Education, as always, is paramount to bringing about discernable understanding to life's complexities. Therefore, it is imperative that we make education the number one priority in America. If we are not careful, the rest of the world will surpass us in their determination to rule the world. We must prepare our students for their place on the global stage of higher achievement. America has the wherewithal to take her rightful stand at the head of the class in the world community. When we recognize education as the major bridge that must be crossed to greater understanding, and human progress, then and only then will we come to bridge the divide that separates us from the goal of peace and harmony.

Education should be seen as a communitywide venture, because the lack of it adversely affects our future. Educators, parents, the community of faith, business, students, and all sectors of the community have a stake in the preparation of our students. When we look for ways to improve our coexistence, we have an obligation to enter into partnership with the broader community with the desire to build cooperative efforts to educate. There are basic tasks that need to be met, such as, tutoring and mentoring students and parents. It is unfortunate that many parents are not qualified to take on the roll as parents, and need assistance to take their rightful place in the lives of their children, Many students are socially deprived, and are not motivated to learn. That is an area of major concern for those of us who are faring better in life. There are teachers who are in dire need of additional in service training in basic teaching approaches, racial and cultural sensitivity, knowing the community they serve, ensuring recreational resources fit into a pattern of educational goals, and ensuring that the curriculum of learning is challenging, but within reach of student comprehension.

All students need measurable instruments to ascertain achievement goals. Many of our students and teachers struggle with the mandated yearly Standards of Learning Test, (SOL).

It may be time to review the effectiveness of spending the school year preparing to pass the test while students suffer from the lack of learning the practical applications of basic reading comprehension, and how to adjust to a complex society. There are many helpful attributes to education that can be brought to bear when we work together for a common purpose.

Other ways to explore just how we can bridge the divide comes from my experience in facilitating frank and honest dialogue between people who have not bothered to become acquainted, while in each others space day by day. We have found, in practice, there is much to be learned from honest dialogue between people who do not look the same, speak the same language, have different outlooks on common interest, and who never leave their comfort zones. This kind of diversity training is a sure way to approach the sensitive subject of race and culture without adverse confrontation, as long as the facilitator controls the dialogue under certain fair guidelines. Training of this nature is usually done in the confines of corporate organizations, and religious assemblies especially where people are drawn. Valuing human differences is strongly advised in this time of increased cultural diversity. There is much to be gained by holding a controlled honest dialogue with mixed cultures. The biggest barrier that stands between us is our lack of knowledge of one another, and those things we have in common beside our humanness. This kind of dialogue should not be limited to the adult population, but is an investment in the future of our youth as well.

During the growth and development years of our youth is the best time to introduce the positive gains of racial and cultural diversity. These are the impressionable years where sensitive issues that cross their lives can make a difference in their total maturation. In order to meet this need, I founded and organized an initiative called the "Student Forum" that was made up of racially and culturally diverse youth in the public and private school systems from eighth to twelfth grades. The students under my guidance organized a planning and steering committee to undertake meaningful dialogue about current issues, and to offer constructive recommendations toward reasonable and positive resolutions. The students discussed nontraditional issues of race and culture, family life, parent/student relations, student /teacher relations, relative school curriculum, and preparing for the future. Race and culture issues were difficult for adults to discuss, while students are not reticent. However, positive differences, and practices were evident in the students after such discussion.

In the observation of racial and cultural sensitivity, it would be good to give some attention to the annual celebration of the "Black History Month" celebration, and critically design relative observations for other cultures, i.e., Asian, European. Latino, African, Middle Eastern, and Others. These celebrations could be reduced to one week, if necessary, but they should be designed for all cultures and races to be enhanced by knowledge or understanding of others. The lessons to be learned are while we don't always see eye to eye; we should respect each other's differences in our efforts to build bridges that will enhance our ability to become closer .

So, we come to a need to vacate our comfort zones in an effort to make this a better land for all to thrive, There will inevitably be inequity in creature comforts, economics, education, and health matters but we can strive to make an effort to respect and celebrate created humanity. Now, let us rethink our purpose for living, and do our bit to fill the social, economic, and religious voids that have gone for want much too long.

Lastly, synagogues, churches, mosques, and other places of religious assembly are natural gathering places for spiritual enhancement around the issues of love and honor. It would be more adventuresome to integrate groups with other groups unlike one another so there is a natural cause for further enhancement, and development of relationships. It is advisable to organize a small culturally diverse steering committee for planning and executing dialogue. Religious groups have a natural ability to draw others into righteous dialogue, because of the basic teaching of faith: Doing unto others as you wish to be done. May God of love guide us to a place of unity.

EPILOGUE

****

I have a deep inner feeling that is cloaked in undying faith and hope that we, as Americans, are witnessing a dying breed of negative and small-minded folk who are still trying to hold onto an antiquated way of life that is drawing to an end. They are being replaced by a younger generation of multi-cultured Americans who have grown tired of experiencing stagnation in politics, religion and superficially advanced education. America has led, participated, and reigns victorious, in too many world events to allow the canopy of racism, hate and division to cause a setback in time. We will move forward with the clear knowledge of what the founding fathers intended. Aesop, the Greek slave of the sixth century, said in a fable, "United we Stand, Divided we Fall." This has proved to be a true saying: similar to where there is unity, there is strength.

It is time to appreciate the existence of other Americans who may not resemble a preferred race or culture, or who may not master speaking the English language, nor adhere to your chosen values, religion or politics. It is the cultural diversity that makes this a great country. The population of America comes from the world around us, and they come to these shores in order to seek a better life for their families and themselves. Unfortunately, that is not the story to be told of the African Americans who came to this land under duress in 1619. However, they too have made great strides in taking advantage of whatever opportunities they found available. Through it all, it can be a greater land for those who are willing to go beyond the status quo and realize possibilities that never have been.

The time has come, ready or not, to take on a new and daring age, where fear of the unheard of becomes passé, and new attitudes of conquest are developed into transformed stages of life. We are destined to move forward into a new world order, because humanity was created to live and grow in productive relationships, and to make this world a better place than what we found.

Evil has its day in the sun; however, man's eventual will to follow his moral compass overtakes evil with good. It always has, and it always will. If the United States of America is to persist, and it will, because we are entering the age of right reasoning, and there is no other plausible path to pursue but the expected dependence on one another.

So let us go forward bound with the grace that can only come from God who espouses good, and shuns evil. We have the opportunity to enhance this earth as was intended by the creator of life. For God's grace in unity to abound, we must be prone to risk escaping from our comfort zones while experiencing the world around us. Now let us build bridges that unite us.

ENDNOTES

****

PREFACE

[1] Sant Kirpal, Ram Dass and the Ram Dass Tape Library. San Anselmo, CA, 1997

[2] Carol Cymbala, Choir Director of the <u>Brooklyn Tabernacle Choir</u>, New York.

Chapter 1

[1] Irene Moore, <u>Ronaald Reagans Evil Empire</u>. World Press, July 2004.

[2] Ray P. Basler, <u>The Collected Works of Abraham Lincoln</u>. Rutgers University, 1953.

[3] Michael O. Emerson and Christian Smith, <u>Divided by Faith</u>. Oxford University Press, 2000.

Chapter II

[1] Sam Walter Foss, (1858 – 1911), <u>Dreams in Homespun</u>, Boston Globe, editor of the Yankee Blade, 1877.

[2] Sigmund Freud, (May 6, 1865 – September 23, 1939). Austrian Neurologist, founder of psychoanalysis.

[3] Samuel Walker, <u>A Certain Defense: Presidents and Civil Liberties from Wilson to Bush.</u> Dr. Walker is professor Emeritus of Criminal Justice at the University of Nebraska at Omaha. The book is currently in production.

[4] L. David Mech, <u>Artic Wolves and Their Prey</u>. Article, National Geographics, 1987.

Chapter III

[1] Edward Gibbon, <u>The Decline and Fall of the Roman Empire</u>. Alfred Knopf, Inc. New York, 1903.

[2] Vine Victor Deloria, Jr., <u>Custer Died for Your Sins: An Indian Manifesto</u>. Norman University of Oklahoma. 1968.

Chapter IV

[1] Bernard Barauch, <u>My Own Story</u>. Holt Rinehart and Winston. New York, 1957

[2] Robert Hayles, Ph. D. and Tom McNulty, <u>Diversity in Corporate America</u>. Bill Dubbs Publisher, Minneapolis, MN, 1966.

[3] Victor Hugo, (1802 – 1885), French Romantic Novalist, Poet, and Dramatist.

Chapter VI

[1] M.R. Watkinson, Minister of the Gospel from Ridleville, Pennsylvania, November 13, 1861. .

[2] Ben Carson, M.D., <u>Gifted Hands,</u> Zondervan, Grand Rapids, Michigan, 1990.

Chapter VII

[1] Ayal Hurst, Creator and Director of Silver Water Retreat, North Carolina.

Chapter VIII

[1] Alexis de Tocqueville, Democracy in America. Two volumes, 1835 and 1840,) Arthur Goldhammer, trans. Oliver Zunz ed.), Library of America, 2004.

Chapter X

[1] John Oxenham, The Hymnal for Worship and Celebration, Word Music. Waco, Texas
1986.

Chapter XI

[1] Joe Darion/Mitch Leigh, The Impossible Dream. Man From LaMancha, 1965.

Chapter XII

[1] Dr. Benjamin E. Mays, (1894 – 1994). Dr. Benjamin E. Mays Speaks. University Press of America, July 31, 2002

LaVergne, TN USA
11 August 2010
192954LV00003B/1/P